Be Careful That You Don't Yoke Yourself Up With An Ass

Cynthia Turner "BabygirlCT"

ROYAL MEDIA
PUBLISHING

Royal Media and Publishing
Jeffersonville, IN 47131
royalmediapublishing@gmail.com
www.royalmediaandpublishing.com

Copyright 2015

Edited by: Claude R. Royston
Cover Creative Direction: Cynthia Turner
Cover Layout: Custom Web

ISBN: 978-0692548905 (Royal Media & Publishing)
ISBN-10: 0692548904
LCCN: 2015953969

Printed in the United States of America

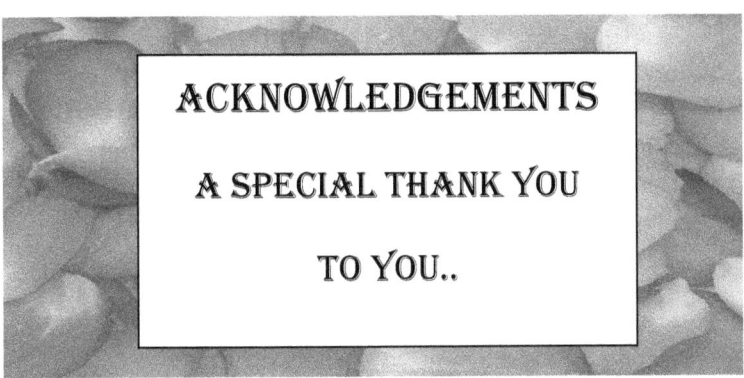

ACKNOWLEDGEMENTS

A SPECIAL THANK YOU

TO YOU..

There are so many people who have been a part of my life. They along with the finishing grace of God have enabled me to get through my life's situations with my sanity intact. I now stand in victory. So, the very first thanks go to Jesus Christ the center of my joy and the sustainer of my life.

To my friends, J.O.T. (my spiritual sister that God attached to me, who knows how to do a little bit of everything on my behalf) she edited this book for me before I presented it to the publishing company. Michelle Stocker (my ride or die sister in Christ) who I once mentored in the infancy of her Christian-walk and now she pushes me and encourages me to walk in my destiny.

A special thanks to my Spiritual Parents, Dr. Samuel Prince Fulton and Mother Dorothy Fulton who always made me feel like I was one of their honorary daughters; gave me the spiritual training that I needed to continue in sound doctrine; and always supported my desire to do things while I was a part of their ministry. My childhood Sunday School Teachers, Mother Zarah Brown and Deacon John Henry Burton, who taught so well and were so dedicated, that they piqued my interest in learning God's Word in my youth. I will never forget my teachings that you provided to me. My current spiritual leaders, Elder George Nash Jr. and Mother Janice Nash, thank you for allowing me the freedom to work in your ministry and cultivate my gifts.

Last, but not the least my publishing company Royal Media and Publishing and Julia Royston who worked with me to finally get this book published.

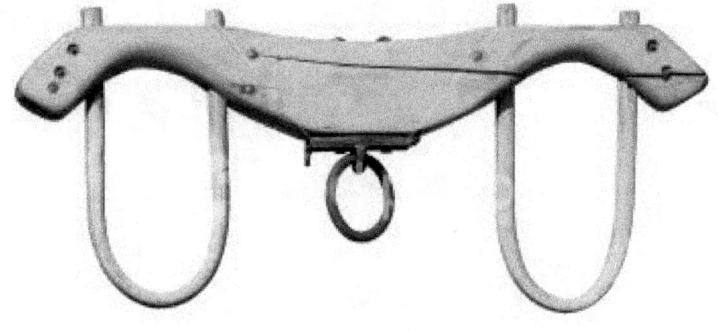

The Purpose

My Pastor asked me what I expected people to gain from this book. What is the purpose? There are so many books written about self-help, beware of religious truths, how to pick a mate, etc. concerning relationships that I just wanted to take it just a little step further. I wanted to go beyond check his/her background, will he work, does he love his mother, does he take care of his children, does he pay bills on time and is he religious? I wanted to encourage people to take a second look and think on marriage and the intricate details that we miss once we have the quote, "basic information" that we were told we need in order to have a successful relationship that leads to our dream marriage.

I just wanted those who care and are concerned about the status of failed marriages and failed marriages in the church to note that we are missing something. In fact, you can have all of the basic information about your mate, crossed every "T" and dotted every "I" and still end up in a failed marriage.

You can match your religious backgrounds with your personal beliefs and still have a failed marriage Why? I will attempt to make you take a second look into failed marriages and the hidden things we forget to search, which leads us to the altar and then to divorce court. Search with me, agree with me and add your own views, because we as religious believers, leaders and individuals have to take some responsibility and initiative in an attempt to ensure that our marriages are based on the right things and that they succeed.

Our churches are depending on it, our families are depending on it, our neighborhoods are depending on it and the generations to come are depending on it. Broken marriages leave broken homes, which leave broken children, which leave broken signals, which leave us broken and confused, which leaves so many broken things.

Are we really prepared for marriage? Are we actually positioned to be married? Are we aware of the sacrifice that comes with marriage and the freedom we are supposed to give up once we become one? Are we ready to become one, unite and stay the course of marriage, no matter what the cost may be? The purpose is also to share with my sisters and brothers in Christ, and to advise them to look beyond the surface and outer exteriors, and to check the character and integrity of the person before you say I do and yoke yourself up with an ass.

Dedication

This book is dedicated to my immediate family.

To my Parents, Choice and Nancy Turner who made so many sacrifices and instilled in me good family values, honesty and integrity to accomplish my goals in life. My heart aches that they went on to be with the Lord before this book was published. They knew that I would succeed because they gave me everything I needed to prepare me for life, so that I would succeed, when they made me go to church. They taught me to treat everyone with kindness, share and to help those who are less fortunate than we were. My father, "Big Daddy" said "help those who help themselves and always pay your own bills. Because one thing is for certain and two things for sure you will always need some place to live." They taught us that a fool and their money will soon be parted. I know they are smiling in heaven with a nod of approval.

To my siblings, Janice, Deborah, Ronald, Joyce, Robert, (Doreen in memory) and last but not the least Steven for always looking out for me and giving me what I wanted even when my parents said no. I dedicate this book to you for every fashion show that you attended, for every drama production that you sat through, whether it was a play I produced or one that I was actually in, for always cheering me on and your overall support in everything that I was a part of from the church to my personal dreams and goals. Thank you.

To my extended family, George Nash, Tyrone Moore and Mabel Turner who have actually been a part of my family for so long that they are considered my siblings, thank you for your support. I do acknowledge that you are one with my sisters and brother and when they have supported me emotionally or financially, you were right there with them cheering me on and supporting me in your own way. Your acts of kindness will never be forgotten. Thank you.

To my inherited son Eric Clanton "aka" Cutabear who taught me how to pray and always had kudo's for his auntie like a mother, who finally made me an Auntie- Grand-mom to Julian Amir Pagotto-Clanton, thank you baby.

To my oldest nephew, George Nash III, who always had a smart comment about my plays (or ghetto plays as he called them and my absolute fabulous wardrobe), but stated he would always be there so when I succeeded I would not forget about him. Thank you.

In Memory, my deceased sister Doreen who although she did not know it, spoke some powerful words in my life, when she told me I was not to have children out of wedlock. She encouraged me to do better, get an education, to make something out of my life and to never let negative people deter me from my dreams.

    To my Godmother, Mary Ellen Andrews for her constant support and confidence in me. For always taking me on vacation, being a bosom buddy to my mother and making me a part of her family. She is the only one who still calls me "baby."

To all of you for the special things you do, I dedicate this book and my success to you.

Introduction

> **Wisdom is the principal thing; therefore get wisdom: and with all thy getting get understanding.**
> **Proverbs 4:7 (KJV)**

Although I have received some male input concerning divorce, this book is solely from a woman's perspective and point of view. The truth must be told and sometimes it comes out as offensive, cruel and disrespectful; but you should know the truth, because it is only the truth that will make and set you free. This book is not a slam dunk or put down against men. God has called man to be the head and the priest of our homes, so we honor them, cherish them and respect them in their rightful places. This book is made up of some of the experiences and opinions of friends and the author of this book, that are within the Body of Christ who thought their marriages would last until death did them part, but they experienced failed marriages. This book serves as a warning sign to people and especially to People of Faith, that believe and think that because they are becoming one with a Christian that everything will be perfect (maturely handled) in their marriages.

There are all types of books written and advice that has been given that try to prepare us and make us look for and at warning signs before we marry, such as:
- Check his family background
- Check his finances
- Check his credit
- Check his religious background

No one has ever said "check his perspective on marriage" (sorry that is not a given or something that we should assume we agree on). Does he really know what a covenant means or what being married really entails? What is his perspective on divorce? Does he feel that once I get in the marriage covenant if it's not working, I can easily get out? If you fail to ask these additional questions you may find yourself yoked up with an ass.

Caution

Judgmental, Closed-Minded People Must Close the Book

This book is only for the mature who choose to learn, share perspectives and hear the views of others who have gone through the pain of divorce. Judgmental, self-centered, self-righteous persons may want to select another book to read. This book is only for the seasoned person who has enough wisdom to learn to crack the peanut – (deal with things on the inside, the good, the bad and the ugly); throw away the shell - (things that do not pertain to them or that they do not agree with); eat the peanut - (digest the things that are good, grow and learn by them). Judgmental, Closed-Minded People Must Close the Book

This book is meant to bless your life, but if you do not follow the caution sign you may find yourself offended to the highest level of offense. If you are not prepared to deal with the unnecessary ugly that occurs in life's relationships and marriages even in the church, you will be appalled by the writings of this author. I hope that this book blesses you, teaches you to grow and learn to deal with the reality of failed relationships and the pain that they so often bring. I definitely pray that this book will help you not to be an inflictor of pain in your next or current relationship.

Be Careful That You Don't Yoke Yourself Up With An Ass

The ring is given and the wedding plans are on the way The one thing a girl dreams of her well planned "Wedding Day" There will be lots of flowers and plenty of frills. No expense spared forget about the bills. The caterer, the food and who will sit where. Oh no you can't sit certain people there. The bride and the groom as tension grows, they fight. She has to have her way she will make it up to him on the honeymoon right. Where will we go for the honeymoon night? He throws a tantrum. I'll plan that if it's alright. The invitations are sent and the day is near.

As they spend time together, they are such a cute pair. Finally, finally it's the wedding date. Who would ever think that their love would turn into hate?

From the Pen of the Babygirl CT

Table of Contents

Acknowledgments		iii
Purpose		vii
Dedication		xi
Introduction		xv
Caution		xix
Poem		xxi
Chapter 1	The Yoke and the Ass The Game	1
Chapter 2	The Covenant of Marriage	11
Chapter 3	Finances – If you have them and don't use them properly	21
Chapter 4	Immaturity – I quit when things don't go my way	33
Chapter 5	Sex – A blessing Not a Tool	43
	Standards on Sexual Morality	57
	Intimacy vs. Sex – What is the Difference	62

Chapter 6	The Proof is in the Pudding	67
Chapter 7	Bad advice – Unwise Counsel	75
Chapter 8	Marital Situations	101
Chapter 9	Abandonment - Should I Stay	151
Chapter 10	Gullible Girls & Belligerent Bad Boys	173
Chapter 11	The Death of a Marriage – Moving Forward After Divorce	189
	Social Gatherings - Group Discussion –	200
	Marriage Quotes	213
	Sneak Preview of the First Lady's Testimony	215
	Suggested Readings	219
	Biography	222

Chapter I

The Yoke and the Ass - The Game

*"As you have seen the treachery of love because of me,
I have seen my cruelty because of you.
But you learned mercy from me, and from you I learned resilience.
As you came to understand me enough to know the value
I placed on selfless love,
I understand your nature better."*
- <u>D. Morgenstern</u>

*"A human being has so many skins inside,
covering the depths of the heart.
We know so many things,
But we don't know ourselves!
Why, thirty or forty skins or hides,
as thick and hard as an ox's or bear's, cover the soul.
Go into your own ground
and learn to know yourself there."*
<u>Meister Eckhart</u>

"The ox suffers, the cart complains."
<u>Victor Hugo</u>

As a Christian growing up, I never understood how Christian marriages could fail. I understood how non-Christian marriages failed because supposedly God was not at the center of their love. Years later and with lots of experience, I am now forced to write about failed marriages in God's Church. So I believe in my heart of hearts that God allowed me to be in his permissive will, so that I could understand and share with my sisters and brothers how Christian marriages fail (some of this information also pertains to non-Christian marriages). Let me first inform you that I believe that it is never God's will for marriages to fail, but that we in our gentle selves tend to select mates who appear to be one way, but after the honeymoon we see the real man or woman (that was oh so well hidden). While one person is pursuing their love and plans for their future with a life partner, the other person is playing "The Game" I will pursue and if it doesn't work, I will just leave—no strings attached.

Before we can talk about a **Yoke** and an **Ass** we must be able to define the terms so that while reading, we can understand and interpret the message given.

- **Yoke** – a frame designed to be carried across a person's shoulders with equal loads suspended from each end. "A joining together to work", to join securely as with a yoke; bind to force into heavy labor, bondage or subjugation; to join or unite.
- **Ass** – A vain, self-important, silly or aggressively stupid person.

The fairytale is that we as Christians will live happily ever after, of course, because we both love God and we are Christians. **WRONG!!** I will never slam the happily ever after theory because I actually know some people who have been married for years and they are happy. There is a small percentage of marriages that are actually working (with no hidden behind the scenes misery) and I personally applaud them. The other percentage have the yoke of marriage on them for multiple reasons; in the church, some stay married because:

- Their leaders tell them that divorces are not from God (and I agree) but we must search the scriptures concerning our individual situations. **(Since God loves and adores you he would**

never want you to stay with a man who is always beating on you, or a man who wants to sleep with other men).

- Pride, they can't let anyone know that their marriage did not work.
- It's better to be miserable than alone, some people stay because they fear they will not get another mate.
- Sex, a little sex is better than no sex at all (**since we are believers, we try to practice abstinence concerning sex outside of marriage**), so I will stay because I have needs.
- The children, we don't want the children to grow up without both parents. (We affect the quality of our children's lives and understanding of our religious beliefs, when we allow them to be a part of our bickering, feuds and fights). **Staying in a marriage for the convenience of having both parents in the home also distorts our children's view of marriage.**

We toss the scripture around loosely that states, "Therefore, What God Has Joined Together Let No Man Put Asunder" Mark 10:9, when in fact God had nothing to do with a large portion of our marriages. We marry for multiple reasons:

- Tired of being alone, "just can't handle the lonely life any longer" I want companionship.
- Sex – Lust, my flesh is killing me, I need to be sexually fulfilled! So marriage becomes my quick fix to mask fornication and ease my sexual desire.
- Finance, I am tired of struggling to pay these bills by myself, so I need a help out. Two incomes are better than one.
- Family, my biological clock is ticking. I don't want to have children out of wedlock; I need to start my family before I get too old.

We can be deceived when our emotions become noisy. Noisy emotions cause us to react to what we see now, in the present, what is going on. So in pursuit of our happiness and to be a blushing bride, we can check all of the signs we were taught to look for: does he have a good job, if he has kids, does he take care of them and participate in their lives, is he a Christian, does he love his mother and treat her well because if he treats his mother well, you know he will treat you well?

Some of the questions that we should ask or teach people to ask are:

- He's a Christian, but does he believe and practice the Bible from Genesis to Revelation?
- He has a good job, but does he know how to handle his money?
  - Does he tithe to the church to help aid the ministry, which will in turn bless his home?
  - Does he tithe to himself (put monies away for the future)?
  - Does he pay his bills or does he just blow money and always have the threat of evictions and turn off notices?
- He loves his mother, but is the love genuine?
  - Is she highlighted and special because she gives him his way and still partially takes care of him and has failed to help him become a responsible man?

If he wants to be married, does he understand the covenant of marriage and the sacrifices marriage entails? I believe that counseling is very important when it comes to marriage. Certainly, if counsel is done properly, you will be made aware if you are about to yoke yourself up with an ass, a prince or your God given king. Sometimes leadership takes you on these long counsel journeys, when what they should address is:

- Do you understand what marriage is about and your duties to a mate in accordance with what the Bible says and not what society says?
- Are you financially able to take care of a home?
  - If not, have you notified your mate honestly of the provision that you can make for her?
- When blended families are involved (both of you or one of you enters the marriage with children) do you have a plan concerning them?
  - Have you put monies to the side for their college education – where applicable?
  - Do you have insurance on the child/children in case of an untimely death?
  - Do you understand that once you are married, your spouse comes first and you should have a financial plan for her in case of your untimely death?
    - ❖ Yes you should have insurance for your wife to bury you, and money set aside in case of your demise.

- - She should not be stuck with the hardship of burying you (and taking on your additional expenses and personal debts).
    - ❖ Just an FYI for every woman/man, you are aware that when your spouse dies you are liable for his/her debts. (financially prepared or not)
  - o Your children should not be allowed to interfere with your marriage.

- Sex: do you understand what the Bible says about sex? You are not to defraud one another. No immature fall-outs and practicing abstinence because you can't have your way. Your body is no longer yours, it belongs to your mate, so you cannot deny your mate. (Please do not take your body is no longer yours out of context). It means that you have connected yourself through covenant. When this is done, you give an unspoken request and desire to please one another sexually. So, in that essence, your body is not your own.

- Discuss what is honorable to you when it comes to sex. (Remember, in most cases, adults have experienced sex with other people and we cannot infringe our previous sexual encounters on our mates).
  - ❖ We should talk about what sex is, what it means, and what we expect of each other. **(Although we were taught in the church of yesterday, not to make provision for the flesh and to shun the very appearance of evil {not that sex is evil} we avoided talking about sex. I would advise you that sometime after the engagement and before the wedding to discuss sex in detail).**

My sisters, my fear is that if you don't get these questions answered truthfully and correctly, you become a part of the game.

The Game. He doesn't really want you, he wants the image of you. He wants to see if he can get you just because he can. Sometimes he doesn't have a clue himself, but he knows he wants to be married for his own reasons. We tend to think, depending on our age, that the boy catch a girl, get a girl, game is over in the church. Contrary to popular belief, the game is still on and that's a sad thing. This fact forces us to go deep to really realize that there are plenty of brothers in the church who are under-developed. We have to remind ourselves that everyone in the church is not sold out to Christ; thus, the problem begins. Even when they have sat in the church for a long period of time, they were never delivered, so when we marry them we find ourselves yoked up with an ass.

Chapter II

The Covenant of Marriage

We must say to ourselves something like this: Well, when Jesus looked down from the cross, he didn't think, I am giving myself to you because you are so attractive to me. No, he was in agony, and he looked down at us - denying him, abandoning him, and betraying him - and in the greatest act of love in history, he STAYED. He said, "Father, forgive them, they don't know what they are doing." He loved us, not because we were lovely to him, but to make us lovely. That is why I am going to love my spouse. Speak to your heart like that, and then fulfill the promises you made on your wedding day."
<u>Timothy Keller</u>
<u>The Meaning of Marriage: Facing the Complexities of Commitment with the Wisdom of God</u>

Marriage has a unique place because it speaks of an absolute faithfulness, a covenant between radically different persons, male and female, and so it echoes the absolute covenant of God with his chosen, a covenant between radically different partners.
<u>Rowan Williams</u>

Do we really understand what covenant means? When we stand before God and all of those people witness those famous words we say: "I do" or "I will" UNTIL DEATH DO US PART, do we really understand the magnitude of the agreement we are making? What is a Covenant?

- A covenant is a binding agreement, formally sealed agreement or contract.
    - Although the word contract is listed in the dictionary's definition of covenant, it is not a part of the biblical definition.
- With a contract, if one agreeing party does something in violation of the contract, then it is considered broken. The whole contract becomes null and void. Basically, the signers of a contract agree to hold up their end as long as the other person holds up theirs as well.
- With a covenant, both parties agree to hold up their end **regardless** of whether the other partner keeps their part of the agreement. A violation of a covenant by one party does not matter as far as the other party's responsibility to continue to do what they agreed to do.

- Covenant in biblical times was God's promise to the human race.

Marriage defined by the dictionary:

- The formal union of a man and a woman, typically recognized by law, by which they become husband and wife.

Marriage is instituted by God according to Genesis 2:18-24.

It was not God's intention that man would be alone. He gave man dominion over everything, the field, the animals and Adam named all of the animals. Did you notice that God gave man dominion over everything but he never gave him dominion over man???

Dominion defined by the dictionary:

- Sovereignty; control
- The territory of a sovereign or government

You may say what does this have to do with covenant? Everything, before we can enter into the covenant of marriage, we must be aware of "Key Terms" that may tear up a marriage.

The perfect example is males and females who take the term "subject" out of its correct definition. God made woman for the man. She was made to be a support and a helpmate for man(see KJV Gen.2:18). She was not made to be under his feet, subservient to him, someone to be walking behind him, or his slave.

Marriage should be a permanent bond in accordance with Matthew 19:6 (any biblical version you would like to use). So they are no longer two, but one, therefore what God has joined together, let no man put asunder or separate. The scripture tells us to be one. We miss the binding covenant, when we fail to become one. It is that societal thing that has entered in the church that causes us to be individualized. Those secular terms "God Bless the Child Who Has His Own", "Ain't Nothing Going on But the Rent", "No Finance No Romance", "If You Can't Pay You Can't Play", "What's Love Got To Do With It" and so on, so many clichés and statements that break our oneness.

We listen to only part of the vows; marriage is not to be entered into unadvisedly; we are gathered here today to join these two in holy matrimony. We promise to love, cherish, honor and obey. We express that the rings are symbolic of our love to each other and explain the circle of love and that nothing or no one should enter or break our circle.

As a part of the curse for mankind's disobedience, God informed Eve that her desire should be to her husband and that he should rule over her. I would not dare engage with the reader and the male species about what was meant when God said that man should rule over her. She should also have trouble in childbearing. God also informed man that as a part of the curse for failing to obey him, he would now be responsible to work. He did have a job but remember that was with ease before the fall. Now, he must till the ground and work for provision for his family. Future corporations now work weeks with others managing them.

Society is slowly creeping in the church defining things to God's people. This should never be, as <u>God left his word for us as our guide</u>. The world is slowly trying to change God's Covenant of Marriage, but the world's view should never be regarded by the saints, (God's Bible believing and practicing people). God has given the Christian clear rules and regulations concerning marriage and this should never be changed, **<u>even if the laws of the land change for convenience, God's Word never changes</u>**. It is still a biblical fact that man should leave and cleave according to Matthew 19:5 and a woman's desire should be to her husband and he should rule over her (Genesis 3:16). Wives should be subject and submissive to their husbands (Ephesians 5:22) and husbands should love their wives as Christ loved the church and gave himself up for her (Ephesians 5:25).

- ❖ If we could get man to perceive this scripture, the unconditional love that Christ had for the church, there probably would be no divorces in the church.

Marriage is honorable in all and the bed undefiled. I thought I would just let you know that we are not to have sex before the covenant of marriage. Yeah, yeah, it's old fashioned but it is still God's word and a part of the covenant of marriage. You would be surprised at the respect and admiration your man will have for you when you make him wait.

In my heart I believe that when we understand the scriptures and what marriage entails that we will not have as many divorces/failed marriages in the church. When we take time to rightly divide the scripture as the word of truth and lean not to our own understanding or quote the scriptures out of context for our own convenience, we will fight to make our marriages work. Let's deal with the terms that we have used and allowed our own understanding to misinterpret and even take a strong stand on:

To Be Subject:

- ❖ To be subject is not to be subservient or beneath but it means:

    Being in position or in circumstance that places one under the power or authority of another

Rule Over

- ❖ Rule over does not mean that a man should be controlling, manipulative or superior to a woman but it means:

    That he should take his rightful place at the head of the family and be able to manage them, as the head and as their covering

When we get it right and understand what love is according to the Bible and not Hollywood's definition, we will understand what Paul meant in I Corinthians 13: the love chapter when he gives us the attributes of love.

Look at the scripture and what would be basic definitions in connection with marriage.

- ❖ **Love is not above but along with**: does not exalt himself/herself higher but is equal and along with his or her mate

- ❖ **Love is patient and kind**: not quick to fly off the handle but is gentle

- ❖ **Does not envy**: is not jealous of your gifting and talents

- ❖ **Does not boast:** does not find oneself thinking he/she is better because he/she may have more things or giftings than another, a verbal put down

- ❖ **Is not proud**: realizes that gifts come from above and is not puffed up

- ❖ **It is not rude**: considers others and does not disregard people, places and things

- ❖ **It is not self-seeking**: not always concerned about one's self and what's in it for you

- ❖ **It is not easily angered**: does not get mad quickly about any little thing

- **It keeps no records of wrongs**: does not remember and record in its mind mistakes made

- **Does not delight in evil**: is not glad when bad things happen to you

- **Rejoiceth with truth**: is happy with what is right and when lies are exposed

- **It always protects**: covers you in every situation

- **Always trusts**: has confidence and believes in you

- **Always hopes**: believes in the best even in spite of things going wrong

- **Always preserves**: fights for what is right to keep what one has

- **Love never fails**: despite all of the pain and disappointment, it remains

God gave Adam dominion over the earth and the animals, and recognized that there was no mate suitable for Adam. So he put Adam to sleep and from his rib, he created woman, a man with a womb. God continued his plan with mankind. Adam and Eve would marry, become one, produce children (be fruitful and multiply) and replenish the earth.

Thus, we must understand that the covenant of marriage is between a male and a female, a woman and a man, and that was God's plan. The union between male and female is the only way we can procreate (bring forth life through childbearing). Everything Adam and Eve needed was already within them. Although skeptics state that there was no marriage ceremony between the two of them, God instituted and deemed them married with instruction on replenishing the earth.

The Bible does not give the spoken detail of sex between Adam and Eve, but when the scripture states that Adam knew Eve and they bore a son (it's safe to say that they had sexual relations), which allowed them to be in the will of God and doing as he commanded.

Chapter III

 **Finances**

*"A foolish man throws his money away,
without planning or planting,
without saving or sowing,
but believes in his heart
that it will return unto him increased
without works."*

<u>Cynthia Turner, A True Life Lesson</u>

Be Careful that You don't Yoke Yourself Up With An Ass"

*A feast is made for laughter, and wine maketh merry: but money answereth all things."
Ecclesiastes 10:19*

No matter what resource you use, the internet, the polls or today's magazines, there is always an article on finance. Finance is always considered one of the top 5 reasons why marriages fail. We teach our daughters to make sure they marry a man who can afford to take care of them. Yes, even in this modern world engulfed with secular information and opinions up to the roof, where independent women stand up and say, "I don't need a man to take care of me, I can take care of myself" we still encourage our daughters to make sure they get a man who can provide for them.

We use to teach our sons that they were the head of their homes and they should be able to provide for their families financially, which meant in that day and time, they should be able to provide a home and the basic necessities for their families. Somewhere between Women's Lib and I'm Every Woman, that teaching was widely lost. Sorry, even in the church, those teachings are now argued and debated. The teaching is debated by women who have become powerful, influential and financially wealthy as well as put in spiritual leadership positions of the Pastorate and the Bishopric. The teaching is also argued by men who have been lost in the financial woes of "but and because" the woman is now making more money than I am, she should do her part and plus take on some of my responsibilities. Women picked up independence and started proclaiming all a man can do for me is give me a good sexual encounter. (WOW, isn't it amazing how the tables have turned)? Of course, our sisters in the church, as we learn the scriptures, no matter how above the man we are financially and how well established we are in our personal lives, we must become interdependent.

Somewhere between the fall of man and the opinion of society, the roles switched and the plans changed and the biblical perspective was overlooked. We started abiding by societal changes and not by what Big Dad and Big Mom taught and showed us, which was usually grounded in biblical principles. We were always taught biblical principals in the Black community because our foundation was grounded in our God. At one time during slavery, God was all we had so we constantly looked to him for provision. When societal changes came, our family values went out the window and we kind of started mixing our opinions and views with the Bible. So sometimes we now have poor attitudes about marriage because of finance.

❖ Case in Point

A woman will overlook an average looking man who would love, honor and cherish her because he doesn't have swagger(or the slang word "swag") and all of the glitter, the fancy car, designer clothes etc., but he could have plenty of money in the bank and know how to handle his finances.

She will pick the good looking man, with the Mercedes Benz, who appears to have it going on financially, but he doesn't know how to treat a woman. Nor does he handle his finances well, which will in turn cause her not to be treated so well, since she chose the outer appearance.

You may be wondering what does this have to do with marriage, divorce or finance? My response would be, everything! Romans 12:2 in part, tells us to "Be not conformed to this world but be ye transformed by the renewing of your mind." When we start viewing things in the flesh and based on what society says, our views become distorted. Believe it or not, this will affect our choices and like it or not, our choices can and will affect our finances.

Finance in a relationship entails a lot and it should be discussed in depth. If not, you will find out how different your views are **after the fact,** and then realize that you've yoked yourself up with an ass. There are times when you can read a book like this and feel that this does not apply to you at your age. You may think this is for silly young girls who view things differently and from a fairytale viewpoint, but the best of us can be deceived. We find out the truth once we say, 'I do.' It appeared that he could take care of you because he had a good job. A man who has a good job and manages his money poorly is less than a man who has an average job but manages his money well. Have you ever asked yourself how certain people can make it and seem to go everywhere and do everything with their little incomes, while others just seem to be scarcely making it, when they may make two or three times more than others?

My crazy girlfriend used to say, "Cyn, people think we have money because we make poor look good." In other words, we are so fabulously dressed, hair in place (most of the time), draped in diamonds (that were purchased on sale with a 50% coupon, and an additional 15% off if we came on a certain day, and then another 10% off if we put it on the credit card) and our I Am Every Woman Phenomenal Attitudes, we look like money. Sisters, we have to stop looking at financial outer appearances and question and start paying attention to how well he handles his finances. If a man brings home about a $1,000.00 a week, buys a pair of snake skin shoes on sale for $400-$500 every other week, loves jewelry, eats out for lunch and dinner every day, wines and dines you in the best restaurants and buys you expensive gifts every week, I can guarantee you that he lives from paycheck to paycheck struggling to pay his bills (unless he is a trust fund baby or has money stacked from an accident). He looks the part but he will cause you to drown financially.

You have to ask yourself, how well does he handle his money?

- Does he make tithing a priority; does he even believe in tithing

- Does he pay his bills on time (this is a credit issue and can stop you from buying your dream house or car with him)
- Does his out-going expense exceed his income
- Does he spend money foolishly by trying to play Big Willie to others when he can't afford it
- Is he always juggling with no excess to save (you must be aware that jugglers will try to make you responsible to financially cover their foolishness)

No matter how intelligent we are or how street smart we think we are, we can be fooled by what appears to be. It is important that you not just talk about finance but that you sit down (don't let him/her just tell you what they can do, but look at it on paper, via pay stubs, current bank statements and tax returns) and discuss things in detail. You may say come on, where is the trust factor? It's back there with those divorced sisters who had it going on before they yoked themselves up with an ass. They now have to fight to keep the houses they put the down payments on and paid the mortgages on for years before they married. The trust is with the women whose credit is so bad that they can't buy a piece of gum on credit. The trust is with the women who had the perfect Coca-Cola shaped bodies and no children, who are now a little oversized and fighting for child support. Need I go on, or do you get the picture? This is horrible to have to say, but I didn't discuss a lot of details on the Game in Chapter I because I didn't want that to be the focus of the book. There are still a lot of games being played. I just don't want you and your sanctified, I believe God self to get caught up in the games and later find yourself to be one of those old, miserable, mean biddies in the church, spitting your venom on the young pretty girls because you were deceived, hurt and have become bitter right in the church. Wow, all of this under finance!

Back to the financial situation, because societal dictates have come into our worlds, our homes and even in our churches, outlooks about finances have gravely changed. Men now look at women as their equals when it comes to finances, when it's convenient for them. We now have the 50/50 rule, which says no matter what happens or who makes the most money, you put your 50% and I will put my 50% and that will make our 100% for our happy home. When this happens, most women start to look at men in a different light. Why?

Because she no longer feels wanted, but needed. You need her to pay 50% for you to obtain the things you want. Go ahead, brother, argue your point. Why would you state from the beginning of a relationship that if she doesn't have her half then it won't work? Women, why would you want a man who tells you from the door to bring your half? God put things in a different order. Man should work and be the head; woman should take care of the home and the children. That's ancient, right? What man is solely providing for his family and what woman is taking care of the home in this time and day? That is why our homes are so out of order because we are out of order; finances cannot always be the priority of things.

I personally believe that according to your household finance and personal goals that both a woman and a man should work. However, when a man makes your worth to him 50%, you have to question where he is financially because he's telling you there will be no joining together if you cannot bring half, your 50%, to the table. When money becomes priority, our priorities definitely change. While there are still some old-fashioned, Bible believing brothers who want to provide for their homes and families, the scale is pretty much tipped to the other side when a woman has to become his equal. So basically, not all, but most of our homes are in a wreck. The house is not as clean as it should be, the children are definitely not as mannerable as they should be, because we can't work, clean, have the babies, take care of the babies, take care of the man, make him feel like he is king, take care of ourselves, stay fabulous, bat our eyes, and then be up and open for a full night of sexual passion in a moment's notice.

Again, what does this have to do with finance? I was hoping you would get the picture by now. That when our finances are out of whack, it can cause a tailspin and wreak havoc on our families and surroundings. Finance can send us into the obsession of obtaining things. We buy things we do not need and have to work, work, work and work to pay for them. While we are working so hard to obtain things, not necessarily things that we need, who is raising our children and taking care of our homes? Where are our children getting their values and development from? Is it from Sex in the City, Reality Shows, Rappers, Musical Talents and Negative Images? This was not God's intention for the family. In most cases—there are some exceptions—children practice what they see. If they see you handle your money foolishly, they will most likely grow up to handle their money foolishly. Believe it or not, finances affect so many other areas of our life. "Man's happiness does not lie in the abundance of things he possess" (the author's paraphrased scripture St. Luke 12:15). So don't just get possessions, let's teach our children real values and principles. So be careful how you handle your finances because it is a true fact that finances can destroy marriages and families. Make sure you check out his finances, the assets and the liabilities before you say, 'I do.'

Notes for Your Thoughts

Chapter IV

Immaturity I Run-Away (Quit) When Things Don't Go My Way

*"Immaturity tears up businesses,
friends, families and countries.
It usually grows
up when everything is destroyed."*

Cynthia Turner
<u>Be Careful That You Don't Yoke Yourself Up With an Ass</u>

*Obstacles don't have to stop you.
If you run into a wall,
don't turn around and give up.
Figure out how to climb it,
go through it, or work around it."*

Michael Jordan

"If you quit once it becomes a habit"
"Never quit."
Michael Jordan

Immaturity is defined

- ❖ As not fully developed,
- ❖ Acting in a childish way: having or showing a lack of emotional maturity

Things that make you go hmm… Immaturity, the fight that never ends until one grows up and reaches a higher level of maturity. People never consider immaturity as a reason that marriage fails. I believe that immaturity is one of the major reasons marriages fail. Immaturity helps tear marriages apart because immaturity never admits:

- Okay, I was wrong and I'm sorry.
- I thought I could do it but I realize I can't.
- My financial status is pretty bad and I need to admit that I am not good with or at handling money.
- You are better at certain things, so I need you to handle it no matter what society says.
- It is my fault.
- There are consequences for my actions and every action causes a reaction.

- I'll be the bigger person for the success of our marriage.
- Running away never resolves anything.

You can't even imagine how many marriages have failed just because of immaturity and pride.

❖ Pride goeth before destruction and a haughty spirit (immature – high-mindedness) before a fall. (Proverbs 16:18 KJV)

This scripture pertains to a person who is above themselves in pride, but it can also refer to the immature person. An immature person will bust up a marriage before they will admit that they were wrong about something. High-minded in their thinking because they could never be wrong, they will let their marriage fail; simply to prove an unwarranted, un-purposeful point that, at the end of the day, means nothing and can cause their marriage to be weakened.

Immaturity causes so much confusion and frustration in a marriage that usually one person will throw a tantrum and walk out, never intending to end the marriage but just trying to have their way about a situation. While, on the other hand, the other person is so frustrated that they make the decision to prematurely end their marriage. The tantrum thrower will always try to get his/her way. In an attempt to try to make the marriage work, the other mate will allow them to have their way and give in to their request. We all must admit that this gets old pretty fast. Once the person who gives in on a constant basis realizes that they are being manipulated, they usually withdraw from the marriage and start going solely through the motions. When manipulation occurs because of tantrums and immaturity and one partner withdraws from the marriage (although they are still there going through the motions) that is the beginning of an unspoken divorce. We are always told to be the bigger person so that our marriage will last. Consequently, being the bigger person can cause you to lose yourself, then right around the corner lurks a low self-esteem and a poor self-worth. Marriage is ordained by God, but it was never God's intention for you to lose yourself, but rather to merge together and the two shall become one flesh.

Before we are married, we always look for signs that will be marriage breakers. Unless the immature person is just a spoiled brat, immaturity can hide itself in the bliss of dating, gift giving, and oh the love! Rarely when you are dating (depending on the age of the person you are dating) will you see a grown man throw a tantrum. They are usually proving to you how manly they are and that they are positioned to take care of you. Immaturity hides itself in males (remember this is from a woman's point of view) for two main reasons; there are others but the main two reasons are:

- Immature males hide their immaturity in their masculinity
    - They look the part – buff
    - They dress the part
    - They talk the talk but cannot walk the walk
    - They can fake it for a moment but it soon comes out that they are not the person they made out they were and wanted you to believe they were
- Immature males hide their immaturity in their ability to feel superior (usually because they have a special gift, singing, preaching or

whatever their gift may be) and to manipulate people, as a result of their own insecurity.

- They hide it well but the reality of the matter is that they feel women are beneath them (their justification is that the Bible says that women are the weaker sex, because in Genesis it was the woman who was beguiled and deceived) but they will never admit it.
- It is apparent that when you speak to most ex-wives, they will confirm how mean their mates were and how they made them feel.
- They treat others mean because this gives them a sense of superiority, power, and makes them feel better in order to hide their own insecurity.
    - These are men who were mentally, physically or sexually abused by a relative or someone who was close to them.
    - Fathers mentally abuse their sons when they tell them what they are not or that they should be like

another person. When they put them down, tell them that they are stupid and that they will never be anything.
- Abandonment by one's father is one of the highest forms of abuse that a son can endure because it creates all types of insecurity in him.
  o Was it my fault that he left
  o Am I not worthy to be stayed with and so on...

(I will not do an open discussion on this matter because it goes deep). It is a known fact that a large percentage of men have been sexually abused by a man or a woman. All of this to discuss immaturity, yes, it goes that deep and this is stuff you can't see on the surface. When abuse, be it mental or physical, is not dealt with it stunts one's growth. It's no wonder that immaturity is killing our marriages; we marry immature, under-developed mates who are put at the head of the family. God does not change his word, the gospel, for anyone, so we still have to acknowledge that men are the head of women. We also have to pray and ask God to give us the wisdom to help our mates become developed (mature) and to deal with the hurt of their past. If we can do this, we can have mature mates. Immature mates tend to hide their failure and make it your fault.

A young lady I am well acquainted with married a pastor who had a handful of members, and he was always trying to put on big programs, such as revivals, concerts, and conferences. He would bring in out of town preachers, singers and special guests, which ultimately cost him more than he could afford, because he had to purchase airline tickets and pay hotel fees. His wife suggested that he use some local people, since his congregation was so small to help defray the cost, which he would ultimately be responsible to pay. Well, to make a long story short, he had the conference, which was poorly attended. The conference was excellent and souls were blessed and encouraged, but he was mad at the world because he thought more of his brothers in Christ would have supported him. He was embarrassed and put himself in a financial strain because he still had obligations and expenses to pay to those invited. So you have to ask yourself what was the purpose? The purpose was that he needed to feel like he was successful at something. In his own little, insecure world he was looking for validation, someone to say you did a good job, he needed some praise from man.

What is the purpose of a helpmate? Had he listened to his wife or even taken what she said into consideration, he could have avoided some embarrassment and the financial strain that he put on himself. Immaturity always has to be right, even when the evidence points that he is wrong. The funny thing is that immaturity never takes responsibility for the wrong or failure that is caused. The pastor turned the situation around. Because he failed to listen to his wife, he made his personal failure her fault. He then faulted the pastors who did not support him or his vision and, of course, he was mad at the world. As a result, he started making more poor decisions because of his bad attitude towards people and their lack of support to his ministry. He became withdrawn, self-absorbed, and started isolating himself.

When a person isolates themself, they only hurt themself, because they become the authority on all of

their plans and situations without another person's view. Remember, two is better than one because they have a good reward for their labor. For if they fall, the one will lift up his fellow, but woe to him that is alone when he falleth; for he hath not another to help him up. Ecclesiastes 4:9-10

Finally, immature persons try to use sex as a tool to get what they want. Not a good thing. You will get the details of sexual power in chapter V *"Sex Is Not A Tool But A Blessing."* Immaturity destroys a lot of things, people and places, but the sad thing is that immaturity usually doesn't grow up until it has destroyed the relationship or when it is too late to restore it.

Chapter V

Sex A Blessing Not A Tool

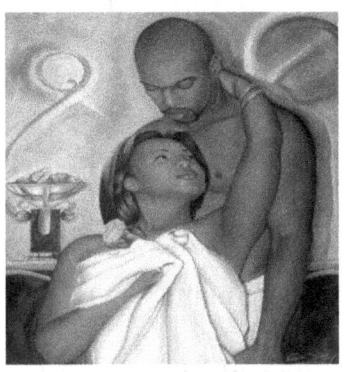

*Set me as a seal upon thine heart,
as a seal upon thine arm:
for love is strong as death.
jealousy is cruel as the grave:
the coals thereof are coals of fire,
which hath a most vehement flame.*
Song of Solomon 8:6

The wife hath not power of her own body, but the husband: and likewise also the husband hath not power of his own body, but the wife

I Corinthians 7:4

Marriage is honorable in all, and the bed undefiled: but whoremongers and adulterers God will judge.

Hebrews 13:4

Christians are bound to sexual purity, so in our ignorance we sometime marry for sex. I just simply need some sex. (See Standards of Sexual Morality at the end of this chapter). God created sex for three reasons and solely for those purposes:

❖ **Companionship**

> Adam was not to be alone, so God created him a help mete/help mate.
>
> So companionship gave him a feeling of fellowship, friendship and relationship.

❖ **Procreation**

> Adam was told to be fruitful and multiply (make babies and replenish the earth) reproduction
>
> Reproduction, the sexual activity, to produce or create, <u>the act of conceiving and bearing offspring,</u> the process of producing babies.

❖ **Pleasure**

> So that man could feel good in his moment of intercourse with his wife.
>
> A happy feeling of satisfaction and enjoyment during sexual intercourse between a husband

and a wife, as God intended it to be for his purpose and his plan.

For all of you stiff people (oh my God she said sex) read Proverbs 5:15-19, study it and understand it, because I will not give you the details or the interpretation of those scriptures.

Although the word sex is not mentioned in the Bible it is implied through other terminologies such as entered in, lie/lay with throughout all the scriptures from Genesis to Revelation. And Adam 'knew' Eve his wife and she conceived and bore Cain and said I have gotten a man from the Lord (Genesis 4:1). Although the word sex is not mentioned, it is safe to assume that "knew" in this scripture is equal to sex. We see all three components of God's purpose and reasons for sex in this scripture.

When people are self-absorbed and a little spoiled, when they can't have their way, they have a tendency to play the sex card. (Women we can probably say ouch right here because I don't know one woman who has not at one time or another played the sex card, to manipulate a man into doing what she wanted him to do). If you make me mad or don't do what I request, I will just withhold sex. (NOOOOO Not the Saints! Yeah Right) the oldest trick in the game, manipulation through sex. That was not God's purpose, for us to use sex as a tool to manipulate. Dr. Myles Munroe wrote a book (I will encourage you to purchase it) the title is "In Pursuit of Purpose." In this book he makes a profound statement that can touch every area of life, from drug addiction, to sex manipulation, to power struggle, to just any type of abuse, be it in the church from the pulpit to the door, a crack house or a power struggle in the hood, he states that "When Purpose Is Not Known Abuse is Inevitable." What a profound statement/quote.

Sex is not a tool to be used for your convenience or to manipulate a person. Sex is a blessing that God created for us as husband and wife. I keep reiterating a husband and a wife when I say sex because we need to know that sex is totally taken out of its place and that is why we have a mess. Now, we have all of these inner struggles in our relationships, because Bey is nowhere near as good in the sack as Fred the Freak and nice Alice is pitiful in bed next to Raunchy Rasheda. What a mess and we have to deal with it. I think this is called ISSUES, and we will talk about this later.

We know in this free sex modern society in which we live, sex is widely abused for multiple reasons:

- Sex for Sale – Prostitution
- General Sex for Pleasure – No commitment (a Booty Call)
- Sex for A Baby – My biological clock is ticking
- Sex for Revenge – I'll pay him back for cheating on me
- Sex for Spite – I'll take your man
- Sex for Perverted Pleasure – Child Molestation
- Pornography, and the list goes on…

Clearly, we can see that when "Purpose Is Not Known Abuse Is Inevitable." Now because we do not understand God's purpose for sex, we have sexual abuse via the internet, rape, cruel and painful sex, pornography, sex-texting and pedophilia.

Sex is clearly and freely discussed everywhere but in the church. I will admit that the church has opened up a little about sex from my pre-teen days in the church and that's probably because of all of the religious sex scandals that are going on everywhere and in every religion. The Apostle Paul warned the married people in

I Corinthians 7:5, not to deprive each other of sex without consent, when they want to give themselves over to fasting and prayer. They were then to come together again so that Satan could not tempt them because of their lack of incontinency or self-control. You see sex was never supposed to be a toy thing that you flaunted in front of your mate, stating look and see but you will not touch if you don't do what I say do. You must understand that your threat of withholding sex could backfire on you and cause your mate to go elsewhere and commit "Adultery." You have to consider the consequences of your action, because you have now caused your mate to stumble, sin and break his wedding vows to you as well as to God. The consequence is not only that your mate has transgressed against God, but that they might find someone they feel is sexually better than you, therefore, creating an additional bind that may cause you to lose your man/woman. The reality of the matter is that your mate does not have to tolerate your foolishness. There is another person lurking in the corridors for a darling mate you just threw away because you could not manipulate them through sex. So, brethren, remember that God has made you the head and you are supposed to handle your business and be responsible for your wife's sexual needs and desires. (Likewise, women, this statement applies to you; it is your job to fulfil your husband's desires and needs). No withholding sex to manipulate your partner into doing what you want them to do.

The consequences of your actions, denying your mate sex, brings up a subject that everyone is scared to discuss or even dare to talk about. What happens when you marry a mate and he/she is a zero in bed, and they just don't please you sexually????? I hear your thoughts. Maybe I'll do a blog to get all of your interesting views. I'm sure all types of controversy and word wars would be started throughout the religious and secular community. This takes us back to the fact that in most cases, before we marry we have had other sexual partners who may have been willing to do things that you wouldn't dare do. (Let me just take a station break here to say that God left us his sexual exclusions in the Bible.)

- ❖ Men are not to have sex with men, vile affections - homosexuality

- Women are not to have sex with women, vile affections - homosexuality
- Man is not to lie with animals - bestiality
- Man or woman should not have sex with a person they are not married to – fornication
- Married persons are not to have sex with anyone who is not their spouse- adultery

In addition, there are laws of the land concerning sex that we must abide by unless we want to deal with the consequences of prison time and they are:

- Rape – sex against one's will
- Incest - sex among relatives
- Molestation – childhood or sexual exploitation of the mentally ill

Although we are taught that sex should be taboo before marriage, you'd better discuss it with the person you intend on marrying. The dos and the don'ts, because if you fail to do so, this could cause serious problems, when you find out that Sexy Sally has slept with the whole neighborhood and you can't even in your wildest imagination know how to please her. Likewise, Seductive Stephen has been pimping for years and he could get the ladies to do any freaky thing that came to his mind and you are not willing to do any of that, so you think.

Did you know that environment and religion can affect a person's experience with sex? If you marry a girl who comes from a strict religious background (not every girl – LOL, because the church girls are said to be the most on fire) she will be straight laced, everything that you want to do to her body is a sin. Don't kiss me there, don't touch that, and you will get a lot of noes. So you will only be able to assume the missionary position with them, straight sex, no variations. On the other hand, you have Loose Lucy and she has been exposed to everything and comes from a very open family and environment when it comes to sex. These are the young ladies whose mothers took them to get their birth control pills when they were fourteen years old, refusing to let them bring another mouth home to feed. These parents think they are helping their children, because they don't want a newborn baby whom their child can't be financially responsible for, thus making them responsible to have to raise and feed another child. These are the girls who have been exposed to everything from swinging on poles to anal and oral sex.

These same women may become Christians and have that sexual appetite.

The church, the leaders or the people in it tend to give sexual advice from where they are and what they have been exposed to, their own personal views on the subject. I remember watching a tape and the preacher was making an undercover joke about sex. He stated that the man got up and said he was married to his wife for 50 years and never saw his wife naked. Wow! I don't think that would work for this generation. Modern men would never allow us to stay covered up on a constant basis and only feel us when the lights are out. However, that must be what he was taught (not scriptural), but nevertheless his view. He must have believed that a man should not see his wife naked in order for him to get up and make that public announcement. Is it wrong to view your opinion or state that a man should not see his wife naked? Absolutely not! <u>Is it wrong to try to make your personal view scriptural? YES!</u> God gave us laws, rules and regulations about sex, so get mad if you will, **if it's not in the Bible, whatever two consenting adults do is their business, not yours. Marriage is honorable in all and the bed undefiled.** In plain terminology and in clear English, it is not the church or the leader's place to tell married people what they can do in their bedroom. That's private; this would be a mind your own business situation.

Make sure you discuss what is acceptable to you in detail before you marry, or you might be walking into a mess if you are going to be close-minded about sex. So discuss your boundaries before you are married. If you know there are some things you are not willing to do, you should be open and honest before you marry him/her to avoid arguments, spiritual debates and frustration. You should never force your mate to do something with which he or she is uncomfortable. Remember, when your mate's pain causes you pleasure, you have moved into conflict and disrespect. This action will usually be followed by an angry partner who will be apprehensive about pleasing you in the future.

Now back to the subject. What do you do when your mate does not sexually please you? The Church Mother (an old mother in Zion, not our new founded church mothers) would tell you to pray. Pastors would fear counseling you (some pastors, not all) in a situation like this because he cannot comfortably tell you what to do, because he may feel that he is crossing the line into your personal life. He has to deal with the fragile ego of the man if it is the woman complaining about sex. Most men would not complain to the pastor or seek counseling about sex if it is the woman displeasing him (again, I am saying most men; there are some exceptions to the rule) because they feel that it may implicate that they are not doing something right in order to get what they want. Instead, most men may seek counseling from a close friend, (male, their homeboys, or female, a friend who is like a sister) who does not always give good, sound advice. The male advice is you are the man, make her do what you want her to do. Or they will make you weigh your options; well, she's a good girl, just go outside the marriage to get what you need. Yes, the carnal brother will encourage him to commit adultery. That's where the quiet rule comes from. 'I make my mistress do in bed what I won't require my wife to do.' His friend like a sister usually encourages him to communicate what he feels to his wife and work on it. The only thing you can do to fix a poor sex life is to talk about it. Discuss what you don't like and try to be open with one another in a calm, relaxing atmosphere and state your desires. There is absolutely nothing wrong with seeking outside help, be it a book, counsel from a professional therapist, or having a physical check-up to see if there is a medical/psychological problem that prevents you from pleasing each other. Communication, in most cases, is the best solution because it could pull out the psychological problem(s) that will not allow your mate to let go and enjoy him/herself and sexually please you. Psychological problems occur when one may have been raped, had broken promises from the trust of another mate, sexual negative connotations, molestation or whatever the problem may have been. These problems may cause your mate to be reserved and not let go sexually. Remember, sex is a blessing and not a tool, so you have to deal with the problems that may have occurred in the past. So don't be so harsh on your mate, a deeper level of understanding will get you a deeper level of desire to please you.

Brothers and sisters, we have to remember that sex is in us. When God made Adam and Eve, it is not recorded anywhere in Genesis that he told them what to do to turn each other on sexually. Adam and Eve gave each other a touch and a look and it was on, he got an erection and her body went into I'm ready mode. The scripture tells us from that point that Adam knew Eve and they conceived and brought forth a son. Sex is already in us, it is natural for our bodies to react in preparation for sexual intercourse. So sorry to burst your bubbles, brothers who say, "Yeah, Doc, she was a virgin as pure as the driven snow until I taught her everything she knows." Sorry, you didn't teach her anything, you just told her your preference. Her body was already designed to give you pleasure. Sorry, Seductive Sally, thinking he was a boy until you made a man out of him. You told/showed him your preference; his erection came with his desire for a woman. So now that we have all of this information, please know that information and knowledge is power, and it is to be used to better your life. In this case, your sex life. Remember, 'Sex is a blessing and not a tool.' If you learn nothing else from this chapter, please remember to NEVER try to manipulate your mate by denying them sex; it will cause problems, not to mention that it is biblically wrong.

Standards of Sexual Morality
The New International Version Full Life Study Bible, Page 1936, notes excluded.

***Hebrews 13:4** Marriage should be honored by all and the marriage bed kept pure, for God will judge the adulterer and all the sexually immoral.*

Above all, believers must be morally and sexually pure (2 Corinthians 11:2, Titus 2:5, I Peter 3:2). The word "pure" (Gk hagnos or amiantos) means to be free from all taint of that which is lewd. It suggests refraining from all acts and thoughts that incite desire not in accordance with one's virginity or one's marriage vows. It stresses restraint and avoidance of all sexual and excitements that would defile one's purity before God. It includes controlling one's own body 'in a way that is holy and honorable' (I Thessalonica 4:4-5), and not in passionate lust. This scriptural instruction is for both those who are single and those who are married. With regard to the Biblical teaching concerning sexual morality, note the following.

(1) Sexual intimacy is reserved for the marriage relationship and is approved and blessed by God only in that state (see Genesis 2:24). Through marriage, the

husband and the wife become one flesh according to God's will. The physical and emotional pleasures resulting from a faithful marriage relationship are ordained by God and held in honor by him.

(2) Adultery, sexual immorality, homosexuality, sensuality, impurity and degrading passions are considered grave sins in God's sight, since they are transgression of God's law. (See Exodus 20:14) and a defiling of the marriage relationship. Such sins are severely condemned in Scripture (Proverbs 5:3) and place one outside God's kingdom (Romans 1:24-32; I Corinthians 6:9-10; and Galatians 5:19-21)

(3) Sexual immorality and impurity include not only forbidden intercourse or consummated acts, but also involve any act of sexual gratification with another person other than one's marriage partner, achieved by uncovering or exploring the nakedness of that person. The contemporary teaching that says sexual intimacy among "committed" unmarried youth and adults is accepted as long as it stops short of full sexual union is a teaching contrary to God's holiness and the Biblical standard of purity. God explicitly prohibits having any kind of "sexual relations with" (literally, "uncovering the

nakedness of") anyone who is not a lawful wife or husband (Leviticus 18:6-30, 20:11, 17, 19-21).

(4) The believer must exercise self-control with reference to all sexual matters before marriage. To justify premarital intimacy in the name of Christ merely on the grounds of a real or a felt commitment to another flagrantly compromises God's holy standards with the world's impure ways and, in effect, justifies immorality. After marriage, sexual intimacy must be confined to one's marriage partner. The Bible names self-control as one aspect of the Sprit's fruit, the positive and pure behavior that is in contrast to immoral sexual play, gratification, adultery and impurity. One's faith commitment to God's will with regard to purity will open the way to receiving this gift of self-control through the Spirit (Galatians 5:22-24).

(5) Biblical terms used for sexual immorality, describing the breadth of its evil, are as follows:

(a) Sexual immorality (Gk porneia) describes a wide variety of sexual activities before or outside of marriage; it is not limited to consummated, sexual acts. Any intimate sexual activity or play outside the marriage relationship, including the touching of the intimate parts of the body or seeing another person's nakedness, is included in this term and is clearly a transgression of God's moral standards for his people (see Leviticus 18:6-30; 20:11-12, 17, 19-21; I Corinthians 6:18; I Thessalonica 4:3).

(b) Debauchery, or sensuality, (Gk aselgeia) denote the absence of clear moral principles, especially disregard of sexual self-control that maintains pure behavior (see I Timothy 2:9). It includes the inclination towards indulging in our arousing sinful lust, and thus is a participation in Biblical unjustifiable conduct (Galatians 5:19; Ephesians 4:19; I Peter 4:3; II Peter 2:2, 18).

(c) Exploiting or taking advantage of someone (Gk pleonekteo) means to deprive another of the moral purity that God desires for that person in order to satisfy one's own self-centered desires. To arouse in another person sexual desires that cannot be righteously fulfilled is to exploit or take advantage of that person (I Thessalonica 4:6 cf. Ephesians 4:19).

(d) Lust (Gk epithumia) is having an immoral desire that one would fulfill if the opportunity arose (Ephesians 4:19, 22; I Peter 4:3; II Peter 2:18 and Matthew 5:28

INTIMACY VS SEX

WHAT IS THE DIFFERENCE

Intimacy is not a happy medium. It is a way of being in which the tension between distance and closeness is dissolved and a new horizon appears. Intimacy is beyond fear.

Henri Nouwen

Intimacy is defined as:

- A close, familiar, and affectionate personal relationship
- A close association with or deep understanding of a place, subject, etc.
- An act or expression serving as a token of familiarity or affection
- A sexual liberty
- The state of being intimate

Please don't confuse intimacy with sex. Although intimacy can be interchanged with sex, intimacy is not sex. Women and some men like the romance that leads up to sex, the cuddling, the rubbing and caressing, the kisses, the sweet nothings whispered in one's ear and the fondling of private parts; the lying in bed and holding each other while they share dreams or just have plain old pillow talk. A female will usually call this intimacy. (If you do the intimacy things right, 99.9% of the time you will get sex), but intimacy is not always equal with sex.

We live in such a dogmatic world, where the purpose of sex is lost and so highly abused, that some people do not have a clue of the purpose of intimacy. This is usually because "they live by the hit and quit it rule" – just pure sex, no feelings involved. Hit it and quit it used to be a man thing, but in this changing society, where the pain, rejection, neglect and hurt has been inflicted on the female, the tables have turned. In this post-modern day where women are making songs like: "Ain't nothing going on but the rent" and "What's love got to do with it" we have to deal with the societal ills that plague our world and trickle down into the church when these hurt persons become converts.

Barbara Wilson wrote an article on Five Levels of Intimacy. This article can be located via Google Website, listed on the Website March 10, 2014. In this article, she states that the five levels of intimacy are:

- Level One – Safe Communication
- Level Two – Others Opinions and Beliefs
- Level Three – Personal Opinions and Beliefs
- Level Four – My Feelings and Experiences
- Level Five – My Needs, Emotions and Desires

For further details on intimacy, please view the website. The views and the opinions of the website authors are not necessarily the agreed views of the author of this book. The information shared are some studied facts and the opinions of individuals. Please do not judge yourself or your life circumstances around the articles. Please do not make marital or relationship decisions around this information, the information is just shared and may or may not be able to help you with your intimacy issues.

Notes for Your Thoughts

Chapter VI

The Proof is in the Pudding

The Proof Is Not Always In the Pudding Because
Puddings Are Now Being Blended With Other Things
And Can Be Very Deceptive.
Likewise Relationships Can Be Deceptive
So Never Base Your Relationship On Outer Appearances
Because It Is the Inside That You Will See Once Married
Cynthia Turner
Be Careful That You Don't Yoke Yourself Up With An Ass

"Some Englishman once said that marriage is a long, dull meal with the pudding served first."

— <u>Julian Barnes</u>, The Sense of an Ending

And be not conformed to this world. But be ye transformed by the renewing of your mind. That you may prove what is that good and perfect acceptable will of God. (Romans 12:2 KJV)

Do not conform any longer to the pattern of this world, but be transformed by the renewing of your mind. Then you will be able to test and prove what God's will is His good, pleasing and perfect will. There is all this talk about "THE WILL OF GOD" no, "THE PERFECT WILL OF GOD." How do you know what His will is concerning a mate for you? We've fasted and prayed about our mate, but yet the divorce rate in the church is still very high. They say that the proof is in the pudding; if your marriage fails, it was not God's will, if it lasts, it was God's will. I can't quite agree with the latter part of the statement because I know some people who stay in marriages for all the wrong reasons, which I may have previously stated. They stay for the children, finance (it's cheaper to keep her), it's better to have a piece of a mate than no mate at all, fear of loneliness, to have a sex partner or because certain religions state that we should stay, and many other reasons. There is another major reason that people stay together that I have not previously dealt with and that is the conditioning of the mind. Momma said, 'As long as he brings home the money, takes care of home and leaves his folly with the other woman outside your home, you stay and take it.'

People who stay in marriages for the wrong reasons live in a dark, cloudy world. They are always miserable no matter how many things they have or how much other happiness is around them. They are very unhappy people, putting up a façade to impress those who are around them.

The Bible does not state that marriage is to make one happy; however, **there should be some happiness in a marriage at some point and time. If not, your marriage of convenience will end in divorce. This is usually what happens when we see people who have been married forty (40) and (50) fifty years and wake up one day and say I want out, I want a divorce.**

I listened to a series of tapes, by a profound television minister (I will not mention his name) that stated, in most cases, marital problems work themselves out over a period of time. (Come up for air, exhale because I know you don't believe that – if this were the case, there would be no divorces, all marriages could just sit it out until things work their way out). I say that if you don't work on your marriage, it will not work itself out, but will bury the problem, which will usually resurface at a weak point in your marriage. I believe that if you do not deal with your problems, they will deal with you and manifest in many ways, but in most cases in some form of sickness. Problems don't just go away. They must be addressed or dealt with or they will surface during arguments, family gatherings and so on. In most marital arguments, when things are not dealt with, you will always hear a mate say, "Why are you bringing that up?" It was brought up again because it was never resolved. Unresolved issues pile up and then one day the person explodes, leaving the other mate dumbfounded and oblivious because of their action.

The proof is not always in the pudding, but it is in the facts of life. We joke about the old television series the Facts of Life lyrics, 'You take the good, you take the bad and there you have the facts of life.' It sounds like a joke but it is a true factor in our married life. Life and marriage are not always easy. We take clichés like how to have a happy marriage, men state, "A happy wife is a happy life," while they are silently frustrated because they are making attempts to make her happy and that action may not be reciprocated. Women state, "It is my job to make a happy home," but they are making the happy home all alone while he may fail to do his part. Sorry, clichés do not make marriages work; it takes two people working together to make a marriage work. The percentage of each mate must be 100% + 100%. (Although it may come out in different dividends and percentages, for different categories and instances, someone must always be giving 100% at one time or another to make it work.)

If there is always one person giving more that 100% on a constant basis, this is going to make for a lopsided marriage, where one person is short changed and unhappy. Just because one person decides to stay in a marriage where they are always giving and never receiving, always sacrificing their self-worth and happiness just to say they are still married is not proof in the pudding or a stand upon statement that this marriage was God's will. This proof is not in the pudding, but it is in your ability to make the marital promise and stay the course (while constantly working on each other's flaws in the marriage covenant and always considering each other's feelings). No one person should always be considered. If so, we will start losing ourselves in the marriage. Losing ourselves in the marriage usually leaves the residue of poor or low self-esteem and bitterness because the person feels like they are the only one giving and trying to make the marriage work.

So, the next time someone causes you to hold your head down because your marriage failed, while theirs succeeded, you can confidently tell them that every situation is different. The proof is that definitely in a marriage, one person is usually the more mature person and tries to fight to make the marriage work, while the other person is usually the ass.

"The proof is not in the pudding but in the circumstances." *So, the next time you make that statement, please consider what you are saying because you may be adding injury and insult to an already wounded person.*

When winning arguments and constantly fighting to be right becomes more important than having a peaceful union, then the victory is often void and means nothing after the fact. Relationships can be difficult and couples always have different situations to deal with. Always invest in your relationship, pray, communicate and be grateful that God has granted you the grace to have a wonderful husband/wife.

At the end of this book, are a list of wonderful, interesting and informative articles to provide more insight on the topics discussed so far. The views and the opinions of each article's author are not necessarily the agreed views of the author of this book. The information shared are some studied facts and the opinions of individuals. Please do not judge yourself or your life circumstances around the articles. Please do not make marital or relationship decisions around this information; the information is just shared to be able to help you.

The Author's View
Top Reasons for Failed Marriages

Finance

Infidelity

Miscommunication/Lack of Communication

Family Interference

Sexual/Intimacy Problems

Religious Differences

Power Struggles

Emotional Affairs

Lack of Appreciation

Un-forgiveness

Turned Focus/Outgrowing Each Other

Time Management

False Expectations

Chapter VII
Bad Advice – Unwise Counsel

Where no counsel is the people fail but in the multitude of counselors there is safety (Proverbs 11:14 KJV)

*For lack of guidance a nation falls
but many advisers make victory sure
(Proverbs 11:14 NIV full Life Study Bible)*

Those who seek counsel from fools and unlearned people will surely fail at whatever they attempt

<u>**Cynthia Turner**</u>
<u>**Be Careful That You Don't Yoke Yourself up with an Ass**</u>

The way of a fool is right in his own eyes, but he that hearkeneth unto counsel is wise. Proverbs 12:15

Hear counsel, and receive instruction, that thou mayest be wise in thy latter end. Proverbs 19:20-2

Advice is defined as:

Recommendation regarding a decision or course of conduct

Information or notice given concerning a situation, business deal or transaction

(**Unwritten definition**): one's personal opinion given about a situation or concerns when asked

Counsel is defined as:

Advice given especially as a result of consultation

A policy or plan of action or behavior

Purpose of Counsel: guarded thoughts or intentions

There are several scriptures I would like to discuss that talk about opinions in the Bible and they are found in the book of Job, 32nd chapter- Job's friends' opinions about his situation.

1 Kings 18:21 "And Elijah came unto all the people, and said, how long halt ye between two opinions? If the Lord be God, follow him: but if Baal, then follow him. And the people answered him not a word."

You may say to yourself, what does an opinion have to do with bad advice and unwise counsel? Job's friends came with their personal views (opinions) as to why he was in that situation. They never considered that it was God's will or just his plight in life. Elijah questioned the people, how long are you going to have two opinions about God? If God is God, then serve him and let him be God, if Baal is God, then let him be God.

Likewise, you cannot have two opinions about marriage. A preacher with a failing marriage was asked by his wife before she went to a divorce lawyer, "Do you want your marriage to work?" His response was, "Part of me wants my marriage to work and part of me does not want it to work." Realizing her mistake and her bad choice of being found by the wrong man, she decided to end the marriage in divorce. In view of the things she endured in the marriage, she realized that she married instability. "A double-minded man is unstable in all his ways," James 1:8. Women and men, you cannot afford to give a person that much power over you to remain standing and hanging in the balance of their double-mindedness. Life is short and your emotions really can't handle the ups and downs and ins and outs of a double-minded person. Double-minded people are unstable in every sense of the word and you are too good to waste your life waiting for them to make a decision concerning your future.

Before we go too deep into personal views, let's get back to opinions, bad advice and unwise counsel. The scripture states, "<u>Where there is no counsel the people fail.</u>" Proverbs 11:14 and this is because we view things one-sided (our side), until a counselor intervenes and makes us see both points of view. **A multitude of counselors; counsel given by a group of qualified persons should provide safety. Therefore, we must consider who is qualified to be a counselor and who we allow to counsel us.**

Are you a counselor because of your experience?

- Are you a counselor because of your training?
- Are you a counselor because of the wisdom God has given you?
- Are you a counselor because you have an opinion that you would like to share?

The bottom line is that we pick who we want to counsel us. For religious people, it usually is a religious leader, the bishop, the pastor, the pastor's wife, or an evangelist. We select them based on spiritual principles or based on the fact that they are Christians or of some religious background. We have a select group of people whom we respect and we will take their advice or counsel, good or bad as if it's the Word of God or Law. Since we are living in the last days and men/mankind, women included, will become lovers of themselves, more than lovers of God, you might want to consider whose advice and counsel you receive and who you consider a religious leader.

I once dated a young man who was not a Christian. I was a Christian, a baby one, nevertheless a true Saint of God. This man was a girl's dream. He didn't look like Denzel and he didn't have the financial wealth of Bill Gates, but he was a genuine sweetheart and he had what this generation would call "swag". A man as sweet as he was had to be God sent (don't you trust the frame; it's a set-up from the enemy of your soul to send you into bondage). Long story short, I dated him for a couple of years and then the marriage question was posed.

Battling with the spirit versus the flesh, because I was totally aware of what the Bible says about being unequally yoked together with unbelievers in II Corinthians 6:14, I had to deal with the emotion of my singleness. So I started justifying in my mind what an unbeliever was (you know, the normal justifying stuff that we use to make the scripture fit our desires and wants). Is an unbeliever somebody who doesn't believe in God? Because my sweetie wasn't a church goer, but he was a believer in God, in his own way, I decided to go against what the word of God said and sought counsel.

Unwise Counsel: I went to a preacher, well-educated and highly respected, and sought my counsel. I said, "I am thinking about getting married and I know that my sweetheart is not saved but…"

The Counsel: I was told that I was strong in God (what a joke, when I was seeking counsel against the Word of God) and that it was believed that I could win him over to Christ. In the counselor's defense, I believe that God permitted that counsel so he could see if I would stand on his word. As I was leaving the office thinking in my heart that I would marry my dream man, the spirit of

God spoke to me, 'I sent my word to counsel you.' Right then and there, I knew it was not God's will for my life to marry him.

Whenever counsel goes against what God's word says and you elect to obey the counsel and not the word of God, you have just set yourself up to be in the **"Permissive Will of God."**

The **Permissive Will of God** is when God allows you in your disobedience to go against his word to get what you think you just had to have. There are so many people who will tell you not to do it, don't be in God's permissive will. Never go against the word of God to please your flesh, because you may not be able to handle the pain and the consequences of disobedience. So many of us have battle scars because of disobedience and some people never recover. Just ask King Saul; for details, read I Samuel, chapters 28 through 31. God has grace and he gives us his loving kindness and mercy on every hand, but some of us can't handle the penalty. Please understand that grace covers us but there is a penalty for disobedience and rebellion against God's word. "For rebellion is as the sin of witchcraft." (II Samuel 15:23).

Counsel and Bad Advice: I Kings 12:1-15
Please read the scripture when you get a chance. It talks about bad counsel and advice. The king went to his council made up of **older, experienced men**. The experienced men counseled him with the voice of reason, wisdom and their experience. They advised him to give a kind answer, informing him that the way to rule is to serve, to do well, to become all things to all men and so win their hearts. He also went to young men for council. The **young men of his council were inexperienced,** haughty and high-minded and they counseled him to handle the request with threats and demands. Rehoboam, in this instance, preferred the counsel of the young men because they were his friends and because he grew up with them and was familiar with them. So he took the young men's advice and counsel over the advice and counsel of the elderly, which in this case was the voice of experience. Later there was a revolt that split his kingdom. There are serious consequences for listening to the counsel and advice of the un-prayerful and self-opinionated persons.

The Counsel of Friends: The counsel of friends has broken up a lot of marriages and has caused havoc in the lives of many.

Girlfriend Counsel
"Girl, I wouldn't take that if I was you. He did what? You need to kick him to the curb for that deed. You listen to your home girl (who by the way doesn't have a man of her own) tell you how to react." No one said nor is there a rule that says just listen and react to what someone tells you to do. You cannot imagine the covetousness that goes on among females, yes, even in the church. Think about your position, married or in a committed relationship, that is heading for marriage. Then think about their position, single with no man or prospects. When taking advice or counsel from a person, you should weigh their situation and the position they are in. Sometimes misery (an alone person) loves company. So I stress, be careful of the advice or counsel that you receive and act upon.

I had a male friend who had a close friend he sought counsel from. His friend was freshly divorced and mad at the world of women. His attitude was negative because of his situation, which was self-inflicted. He was physically abusive to his wife and she tolerated that behavior. He then used her for her position and then finally for her monies. He later just became a total _ _ _ for lack of a better word. He divorced his wife, his choice, and then was angry because she moved on with her life quickly. Anyway, ask yourself, should my friend have sought counsel from this person? The answer should be, no! There is no way he could have been objective. This man was still hurting and no matter how spiritual or deep you may want to be, you have to recognize that "hurting people hurt people". His counsel and advice could not be objective because he didn't even recognize the fact that he was hurt because of his own choice. His wife didn't divorce him, he divorced her (prematurely, of course, and then he wanted to be angry). He encouraged his friend not to stay with his wife, even though he had no biblical reason to leave.

"In the multitude of counsel there is safety." Proverbs 11:14

This is very true! I always encourage people that before they make any major decision to bounce their rationale off or discuss it with some people of a like mind. Never ask your single, bitter girlfriends if you should leave your husband. Never ask people who don't want to accomplish anything if you should pursue a goal such as college, or switch jobs, or buy a new home. They will never encourage you to do anything. Be careful of your surroundings and the people you allow in your space. How can two walk together unless they agree?

Unequally Yoked. The above scenarios are perfect examples of being unequally yoked. You may ask and what does this have to do with bad counsel or advice? Everything; the Apostle Paul was addressing single people and encouraging them to marry within the faith and not to yoke themselves up with unbelievers. Unequally yoked goes into so many other areas. Unequal simply means not equal or of an equivalent value, status or belief.

Webster's definition of unequal is
- Not the same in a way that is unfair: giving more advantages, power, etc. to some people and less to other people for unfair reasons
- Different in number, degree, quality, size, etc.
- Not able to do what is needed

- Not of the same measurement, quantity, or number as another
- Not like or not the same as another in degree, worth, or status
- Badly balanced or matched (an *unequal* contest)
- Inadequate, insufficient (*unequal* to the task)

We can be married and unequally yoked. You want a house; he wants to live with his mother or family members. You want to educate yourself; he thinks school is a waste of money. You want to work in the ministry and sow financial seeds; he doesn't see the need for you to give anything above tithes and a dollar offering. You want to pray and go deeper in God; he wants to watch TV. Do you get the picture? Thus, the title of the book, *"Be Careful That You Don't Yoke Yourself Up With An Ass."* It's easy to yoke yourself up with an ass because, while dating, they hide their real self and feelings and agree with you. The person who said, "You never know a person until you live with them or marry them," was telling the honest to goodness truth, or as they say in the hood, "they ain't never lied."

In conclusion, it's very important that you seek counsel before you marry. Once you marry, if you realize that you missed something and you are yoked up with an ass, still seek counsel. It is possible that with prayer and counseling, your marriage could still work. **Only** if both of you want to work it out. This is my advice to you. Remember that you do not have to receive the advice or opinion of others. If you realize that you have yoked yourself up with an ass and he/she is nonchalant about working it out with you, get out. If you are always giving and there is never any reciprocation or consideration of your feelings, you may want to weigh your options to see if you can tolerate this type of behavior or treatment. You may not want to stay in this type of marriage. If your mate pretty much has the attitude of, 'oh well, this is the way it is and it's going to be', and he/she is not willing to work it out or change some things, get out. I am not an advocate of the get out plan or divorce, but the reality of the matter is that if you stay, you may be wasting your time. Now you may say what about the God Factor; because God can and he will turn things around. That can only work if you have two willing hearts; both persons have to want to work it out. Staying in a marriage where you are disregarded or not wanted can cause all types of sickness, mental and nervous conditions. I have seen so many of my friends suffer medically because of failing marriages. Rejection can torment our minds because you are always obsessing over the why of the matter.

Low self-esteem caused sometimes by the rejection of the mate can and will cause you to:

- Overeat - become fat and out of shape
- Feel unattractive – because you have allowed yourself to overeat and become overweight
- Sickness – because you have become extremely overweight and in some cases obese, which brings on all types of diseases and sickness in your body
- Mental bondage – thinking negatively of yourself, and thinking all types of ungodly thoughts
- Unforgiving – holding on to the disappointment and the hurt that was inflicted upon you

This circle goes around and around and can cause you much harm. You can't change a person if they don't want to change. If they don't understand the covenant of marriage, they will never want to stay and you can't take that on as your fault. From the beginning, divorce should not have been so, but because of the hardness of our hearts and the consequences of pain, sometimes we have to walk away.

Remember, you do not have to accept advice or counsel, but you had better be aware that God is trying to set you free from the bondage that you may be in.

Notes for Your Thoughts

What you should know about Counsel and Advice

Anyone can give you counsel, advice and their opinion, but you need to seek the face of the Lord to be in his will.

Good advice/counsel can land you into a wonderful marriage or situation.

Please note that good advice/counsel <u>given out of season</u> can land you into a marriage from the pits of Hell and devastating circumstances. Timing is everything. It may be God's will for you to marry, but we also have to be in God's timing.

Bad advice and counsel can alter your life and produce negative results.

Don't listen to the opinion of everyone, it's just people's personal views on situations, sometimes it's good and sometimes it's bad.

Be careful who you receive counsel and advice from, especially if you are going to make your life's decisions around that person's counsel and advice.

Never be manipulated through counsel to do what a person wants you to do.

Make sure you receive your counsel from like-minded people, people who believe as you believe.

Make sure the persons you receive counsel from are qualified to give you counsel and their lives live up to the counsel they are giving you.

<u>Never</u> give a person too much power over you and <u>never</u> let people have control over your life.

Always let the final decision be yours, no matter how much counsel you receive, because ultimately you will have to live with the decision made and the consequences of your decision, whether it is good or bad.

You Have The Ring

But Can You Talk About Everything

He Loves You and You Love Him Too

But Before You Actually Say I Do Answer These Questions You May Need to Know

If You Are Rushing And You Need To Take It Slow???????

On the next page is an information article that I thought was interesting and informative concerning premarital questions.

*Please note the articles are copied as listed on the website; the author of this book is not responsible for any grammatical or typing errors.

National Association of Wedding Ministers
Premarital Questionnaire

NAWM encourages all couples to attend premarital counseling/coaching sessions if possible. However, if you will not be receiving premarital counseling, then please read the following questions and answer them with your fiancé. You will be surprised how much you learn about each other and your relationship from answering these simple questions. Have fun, be honest and follow-up with counseling if necessary.

Relationship

- Do you love and trust your fiancé?
- How will you make decisions once you are married?
- How would you handle/settle an argument?
- What do you do if you cannot agree?
- Is it hard to say please, thank you and I'm sorry?
- When you are ill, how much sympathy and attention do you desire?

- How would you handle end-of-life decisions and life insurance?
- How will you relate to in-laws, opposite-sex friends, ex-spouse or children from previous relationships after you are married?
- Do you believe your fiancé will be faithful?
- Can you see yourselves growing old together?
- Is your fiancé an honest and truthful person?
- How do you show each other affection?
- Is your fiancé kind, gentle and understanding of children, co-workers and family?

Finances
- Who will be the primary financial provider in the family?
- Do you support your fiancé's career?
- How will you decide on what major purchases to make?
- Who will pay the bills and keep the checkbook?
- What is your philosophy of giving to your church or other charitable organizations?
- What are your thoughts about the use of credit cards?
- If either you or your spouse lost your job, what budget items would you cut?

- Will you have joint savings and checking accounts?
- Have you created a family budget?
- What percentage of your income will go toward home, car, groceries, utilities etc.?

Home
- Where do you want to live and in what setting would you want to live (city, suburb, small town, rural, plains, mountains, desert, coastal, etc.)

- What do you expect your marriage and standard of living to be like after five years?
- How soon after you are married do you expect to have your home reasonably furnished?
- Will you do your own home maintenance?
- Who will do the landscaping?

Housekeeping
- Who will prepare each meal and what types of food will you eat?
- How often will you eat out?
- Who will do the laundry and ironing?
- Who will go purchase groceries?
- Who will make sure general automobile maintenance is done?

- Who will do general household cleaning and bed making?
- Who will wash and dry the dishes?
- Do you want a pet in the home? If so, what type?

Children and Parenting
- What is your attitude towards children?
- When will you begin having children and how many?
- What would you do if you cannot conceive children of your own?
- What is your view on abortion and birth control?
- Who will be the primary caregiver of your children?
- How will you discipline them?
- Who will be the primary disciplinarian?
- Will your children do chores?
- Will they receive an allowance and how much?
- How will you deal with children from a previous marriage?
- How will you deal with issues at their school?

Social Activities/Church
- Do you share the same beliefs?
- Will you attend the same house of worship?
- What will you teach your children regarding your

faith?
- What hobbies or recreational activities will you pursue individually, together, and how often?
- How will your personal friendships (his/her friends) change after marriage?
- How do you feel about alcoholic beverages, smoking and guns in your home?
- Where will you spend the holidays, birthdays and anniversaries?
- Will you both have certain times to spend with your own friends?
- Will you be joining any social clubs?

Red Flags
- Your fiancé seems to be irrationally jealous of friends, family or past relationships.
- Your fiancé is prone to extreme emotional outbursts and mood swings.
- Your fiancé displays controlling/smothering behavior.
- Your fiancé is unable to hold a job.
- Your fiancé is unable to resolve conflict.
- Your fiancé exhibits dishonesty.
- Your fiancé does not treat you with respect.
- Your fiancé is overly dependent on others for money.

- Your fiancé exhibits patterns of physical, emotional or sexual abuse towards you or others.
- Your fiancé displays signs of drug/alcohol abuse

Note: If any of these signs exist, you should schedule a time to talk with a minister or counselor immediately.

Source: Google, August 4, 2014 - a general list of pre-marriage counseling questions – Reprinted with permission of the Author.

Chapter VIII

Marital Situations

Why do we quit???

It's all situational

"You don't marry one person; you marry three: the person you think they are, the person they are, and the person they are going to become as a result of being married to you." Richard Needham

Marriage Situations

It's very easy for us to judge one another concerning divorces and what happened in each individual marriage. So I gathered some information on marriages that I was familiar with (all Christians) to get some perspective on what happened in these individual marriages and what would be done differently the second time around. The names of the persons in each situation have been changed for privacy purposes.

Situation #1

Lust and Loving Lucious: Wrong focus – Lucious & Lawanda

There was a young lady who grew up loose, so for name's sake, we will call her Lawanda. Lawanda became a Christian but found it very difficult to live holy in her body; she just couldn't get that practicing abstinence thing together. She tried and was almost successful until she met that fine hunk of chocolate called Lucious. You don't have to be deep, prayerful, or even a Christian to know that lust and Lucious would create a fire. From the words of Solomon- Proverbs 6:27: "Can a man take fire in his bosom and his clothes not be burned?"

Definitely not! Praying and playing, she found herself pregnant. Her love for Lucious was deep to the bone and she had to have him. Her friend cautioned her to wait and give him some time to grow up and learn to be responsible. So to circumvent the lust and the burning in their flesh, they married (wrong focus and action). If lust is a problem, marriage will not fix it. It will put a Band-Aid on your temporary passion and desire. You have to fix lust and fight to put it under your feet in the name of Jesus or it will resurface the next time a skirt or pants flaunts past you with finesse or attractiveness.

You see, lust is a spirit with a vicious appetite. Lust will convince you that you will die if you don't have her or him, and once you get the person they become... what. Lust drove Luscious in the bed with most of Lawanda's friends (or should I say associates because a friend would never sleep with a friend's husband) with the exception of one friend. Lust caused him to be a real playboy or should I put it like the Bible says, a real whoremonger. They played a real cover up game. He would rarely work, and why did he have to grow up? I mean, work, when all of the woman he lusted over and had multiple affairs with paid his way and gave him financial assistance where he needed it? The marriage lasted for years and she went through turmoil, mental anguish, and financial struggles.

She woke up one day and realized what she endured and instead of praying, she lusted back. Unintentionally, she found herself so hurt and beaten down mentally and emotionally that she became that hurt person who wanted to hurt back. She paid him back big time. She lowered her standards so low that she did the unthinkable with the unthinkable. Although he initiated or should I say participated in the affairs with other women, while his wife stayed the course, he couldn't handle the big pay back. We have to understand that although we love our spouses, we cannot go against the word of God to fix things or to try to make our hurts equal. Remember the word of God states in Romans 12:19 latter part, "Vengeance is mine; I will repay," saith the Lord. After all of the hurt and pain he caused Lawanda, he just couldn't handle her affairs. So he turned his lust to another woman and finally they divorced. They unintentionally split the children's affections and allowed them to see the ugliness that lust caused.

Life Lessons

- Never marry because of lust
- Although sex is an internal desire it should not rule us as if we have no temperance or self-control via the Holy Ghost
- Marriages built on a poor foundation rarely succeed
- Only God and the desire of both a husband and a wife can allow the foundation of a poor marriage to be rebuilt and placed on firm and fertile ground
- It takes more than a burning desire for you and your mate to make a marriage work

Situation #2

Lies, Lies and Alibis: The Fairytale Story – Bianca & Buster

One young lady, we will call her Bianca for identity purposes, stated that she married a Godly man who did not tell her the truth quite often. We will call him Buster. He promised her the world but failed to come through on any of his promises. The fairytale starts like this: he was a nice young man who could preach and teach that word, the word of God, that is. They became good friends. She thought he was so nice that she tried to hook him up with a couple of her girlfriends. He wouldn't go for that because his intentions were to be with her. Finally, one day he got his heart up to ask what it would take to transition their friendship into a relationship. Bianca hesitantly advised him that she would have to think about it, because he had a busy life. He was previously married, had a family and just had a lot going on in his life. So she pondered in her heart if she should give him a chance and make a commitment to him. After all, everyone makes mistakes in their youth. She prayed about it and then decided to give him a chance.

Well, they had the fairytale relationship and then planned to marry. She shared with him her old-fashioned values and ways. Men are to provide a home, make sure there is a home, and pay the bills. A woman's money should be extra, to help and to provide things that did not fall into the scope of his responsibility. She would cook and clean, take care of him and make their house a home. She advised him in other words, I am the help and not the provider. **(These were her values and he didn't have to agree to them, because that was her standard and if he didn't like it, it was his option to walk away).** He agreed to her values. By then they were engaged. It all went haywire when he was supposed to save a certain amount of money to help with a deposit on a new home and he did not come up with his share. In an outrage because she felt like that was lie number one and he didn't have the decency to convey his situation up front, she broke the engagement. She informed him that he was not prepared to marry her and that they were not little children. When you can't do your part, you have to communicate that, if not, your marriage will be doomed before it starts. If you can't trust, then what do you have?

She went her way, but he kept in touch, proclaiming his undying love. One day, he manned up and explained that he over-extended himself and so when the time came, he wasn't in position to do what he promised. She found out after the wedding that his getting in position was borrowing from anyone who would lend him money without her knowledge. He slid his way back in her life and promised to handle things. She still didn't go for it because she had trust issues and his actions reinforced her lack of trust.

He pleaded and begged her to be with him and to marry him. So she agreed to be his wife, giving him the benefit of the doubt and thinking, *oh, he is a man of God, and with that comes a certain amount of integrity*, so the wedding plans began. He stated that he would take care of the house and the honeymoon, so he put very little to the wedding because he would take care of the other things that were needed.

With no communication about his financial standing, they went on the honeymoon only to find out when they arrived that the hotel was not paid for. WOW. What a way to begin a marriage. In her heart, she started to have the marriage annulled, but she remembered those sacred vows and got over the lie that he was taking care of everything, while she was facing a hotel bill that he could not afford to pay. Marriage Lie #1 was being displayed right before her very eyes. She convinced herself to stay in it. "Holy Matrimony" was supposed to be until death do us part, so she blew it off. They were one, but she was not supposed to be the one having her money spent. So she moved on with her marriage. It was just a situation and she got over it.

He picked the honeymoon location, a tropical island. The honeymoon was a dream. Food for thought, do you think he needed her funds to take his dream vacation? We must learn that when untruths are thrust upon us and it is not communicated to us as to what happened and the why of the situation, suspicion and disappointment lurk in the back of one's mind. This causes us to pay attention to other situations and to feel deceived. To add insult to injury, when it was time to pay the down payment on the house, he just got the dumb look. This situation just screamed liar, liar and lie #two.

Stuck in a mess with a liar, she questioned, "Oh, God, did I miss you?" She then forced him to man up and told him that every dime she put down on that house had better be paid back to her. He did pay it back at the risk of not paying his bills (which she did not know) until she started seeing his bank letters in abundance and realized that he was bouncing checks. Trying to deal with things, she then noticed that this grown man put himself in bad situations and then threw childish tantrums to get his way. "I believe he may have thought this would be manipulation through actions." She was finally forced with dealing with the fact that giving him the benefit of the doubt was a bad thing because he was simply just a liar.

One month into the marriage, he was drowning financially and getting further in a hole. Realizing that she married an immature person, she tried to reason with him about his finances. He was quite the arrogant person, but she forced him to be a man and 'fess up' that he was bouncing checks and getting deeper in the hole.

He realized that his wife took a stand and she was not going to be the head of the house because that's where God placed him. After all, she was very up front with him about her position concerning their finances.

Just as a good wife would do, she jumped in to try to help her man. She paid the mortgage on his other property, the insurance, and helped in some other areas but refused to pay any bills that were made in the house with the exception of the phone bill, the food bill, the cable bill, the internet bill, and for things that were needed in the house. Frustrated and aggravated, she had to deal with one financial woe after another because he handled his finances very poorly. Finally, she couldn't take it anymore because she lived a good, peaceful single life before she married him. She made the decision for them to live in her rental property. He didn't like that, although it would be the answer to his financial woes.

She was furious because she could not believe that after all of the talking they did in preparation for their marriage, he just disregarded everything. He evidently thought that once they were married, she would disregard her standards and just let him do what he wanted to do with her money, which was totally wrong, and knowing Bianca, that would never happen. He broke all of his promises. They never joined together financially (as married people should) so they lived in financial division. He had quiet frustration because he felt like she should always help him with things he said he could take care of before they were married. When things and situations change, what a mature mate should do is come back to the table and confess, "I can't do what I said I could do." Since that was never done, she was always aggravated. After all, she had her own bills to pay and she told him if he wasn't ready and if he could not afford to take care of her, he should not marry her.

Once married, he always needed help with one thing or another. He was arrogant and had no humility. He thought she should just give him her money to cover his foolishness (if you know any Biancas – Sister, Sister, you know that would never happen). Once married, she figured out that he was a juggler, a person who robs Peter to pay Paul. A person who uses money for things other than what they were designated for, which always made him short for cash in other circumstances when the bills were due. The tension and the disappointment caused them to have a big blow out and he threatened to leave her.

She looked around, and everything was hers, the house, the furniture, the televisions, the pots and pans, the refrigerator and the stove. He was a liar and he added nothing to her life. Furious at his nerve, she advised him not to make threats he couldn't keep. He thought his threat would get him his way, but his plan backfired on him. Not willing to go through any more childish tantrums and manipulation, she was kind and gave him grace to stay for a while to allow him to get his finances together. She also gave him a deadline to get out. He now needed to find some place to live, because he broke every promise to her, he lied about everything and he had no decency or integrity. On top of that, he was an immature little boy in a man's body. He failed to cover her as he promised to do. He spent money he didn't have, to impress people who couldn't care less about him.

Finally, the separation that should have made things better and given them both some time to think things over did not work to their marriage favor. They were not working on fixing their marriage, so she requested her house keys from him which devastated him. She realized that her time and money was wasted and that she had to deal with things as they were or move on with her life. She received the call that broke the camel's back. Her husband had bounced a check to a person who did him a favor because of her good grace. He didn't even have the decency after months passed to tell the man that the check was no good. She spoke with him in her state of fury and demanded that he bring her cash to make things right. She was so embarrassed; it was then that she realized you can't give a person integrity, they have to have it down on the inside. No matter how many facades a person may use, they can't camouflage integrity.

It takes two persons to make a marriage work, just as it takes two persons to make a marriage fail. Their one last conversation made her decide to divorce him. She asked him if he cared about his marriage and if he wanted his marriage to work. He stated that part of him did want it to work and part of him did not want it to work. A double minded man is unstable in all his ways James 1:8. He did nothing to fix things or work on his marriage, so she made the decision to end it. He was disappointed and angry with her for divorcing him, as though he took no part in this bad marriage. Isn't it ironic how people in a marriage fail to see their fault and their part in ending the marriage? Yet they are so angry and can't admit to their own self that they did nothing to make their marriages work.

If you are not a part of the solution then you are most likely a part of the problem."

She refused to give him that much power over her in his time of double mindedness. In addition, she had a phobia that he would leave town and tie her life up for years in his time of selfishness. Since she did not want her testimony to be that she had a husband somewhere and they were not together for years, the divorce proceedings began and were finalized.

Life Lessons

- Never assume that your mate has integrity. Make sure his finances are in order and ask questions
- Before you marry, request to see copies of pay stubs and current tax returns (sorry, we are living in a time where you just can't take their word for it)
- Always discuss what his/her outgoing expenses are; this will help avoid the finance arguments and give you a little piece of mind to believe that the person may be able to keep a fair portion of their promises
- Never make threats unless you are intending to follow through with the action (idle threats can end your marriage prematurely)
- Understand that even if you lied to get your mate, somewhere along the line you will have to learn to tell the truth (only the truth can make you free and pull you out of the bondage of the lies that you have told)

Situation #3

Generational Curses Revealed -Freaky Frances and Under Cover Ulysses

This next situation is very deep. It deals with a promiscuous girl (promiscuous being a family trait and generational curse because all of the women in her family had high sex drives, multiple baby daddies, and most of them had a child by another man while they were married) we will call her Freaky Frances. She hooks up with an undercover lust addict who was called to the priesthood and we will call him Under Cover Ulysses. When Solomon says, "Wake not up my love" Song of Solomon 8:4, he was stating let things sleep that should not be alive. Don't wake up that thing in me before time because if you do it can open up a can of worms that you are not really prepared to deal with. So sometimes we have to learn to just leave it alone.

Frances dated Ulysses and they fell in love. She had to have him and he had to have her, so the marriage began. She quickly began to separate and isolate him from his friends so she could have him all to herself.

The longer they were married, she pushed him to do all types of sexual things. She just couldn't get enough because he could not please her sexually, so she pushed him on the other side. Once Pandora's Box was opened, he tried a little of everything and, people, things you could not imagine until she no longer was enough for him. Isn't it ironic how the tables turned; Freaky Frances stated that Ulysses couldn't do enough to please her? When he went over the edge trying to please her, he opened himself up to generational curses and spirits of perversion, which now became a problem.

Sexual compatibility is and can be a problem. I can hear the church mothers rebuking me now, "God Made Woman to Please Man – Sexual Compatibility", is from the pits of Hell and it's something this demonic generation created. Well, while I agree that one of the generations must have started this, if we look closer, it can be traced back to biblical days and perversion as stated in the book of Romans. For the purpose of our discussion, that's not my focus nor will I do a study on it. I don't know who started the sexual revolution and created this freaky stage but it is something that we must address. A large portion of marriages in the church and out of the church fail because of the lust of the flesh, which usually pushes one or both persons into an extramarital affair.

Freaky Frances and Under Cover Ulysses are prime examples of this situation, *sexual incompatibility*. Before you come to your conclusion, hear me out in this reading. With all of the acts that Freaky Frances was practicing on other men, it was her "BC" Before Christ days. In sin, in most cases, not all, there are no limits put on sexual fulfillment. If you think I am not truthful or informed, just go online. No, don't go online; it might expose you to some perversion that you are not ready for and get you caught up in that perversion. Just go downtown to a sex store where they sell all types of sexual gadgets. Better yet, you can have a home show; there are all types of businesses to get you going. Not to speak of the million/billion dollar drug industries that are making a killing telling you how to enhance your sex life via pills and creams. Frances brought the sexual acts that she practiced on the other men into her bedroom with her husband; yes, this was a problem with him that filtered back to her. What do we do when a person's sexual appetite has become a problem for their mate?

"Address the Issue." It's really not that your mate can't please you sexually (unless there is a medical problem, mental problem or an ego problem). The fact is that we are bringing other people in our bedrooms. Hear me out before you close the book. If we can be truthful with ourselves, when we've dated multiple people and when we look back in retrospect, each man/woman had some sexual traits or should I say tricks that we liked. That's where the - If I Could - comes from; if I could take the brains of Johnny, the swag of Keith, the money of Billy, the talent of Lenny, and the body of Steven and combine them all together, I would have my dream man. Wake up and smack yourself. You can't have all of those men in your marriage. Men think if I could also: If I could have a woman with the looks of Halley Berry, the body of Janet Jackson, the intellect and influence of Bernice King, the spiritual wisdom of a mother in Zion, the finesse of Angela Bassett and a whore in my bed, I would have the perfect wife. You can wake up and smack yourself too. You cannot bring all of that pressure and expectation in your marriage and expect it to work. He/she is not all of those people. You have to allow your mate space to be who they are. Freaky Frances will never admit it, but she initiated the problem in her marriage. Her freakiness, which was actually a lust problem and an obsession for an orgasm, caused her mate to go longing for things deeper than she could ever imagine. As a result, they both had multiple affairs, but he took it too far and finally the marriage ended badly in divorce. Again, the children were exposed to all of this ugliness. *Before we marry, we have to take a look within, check our motives and let go of all of the past relationships and even hurts. Find out what's driving you, because if you let the devil ride he is going to want to drive. It's evident that our marriages fail when we let the devil in and then allow him to drive.

When lust enters our marriages, and I am talking about sexual lust, which is not towards your mate, you must search the source of this matter. As discussed in Chapter V, Sex is a blessing not a tool. We have to address what is sexually acceptable before we get married. It was never God's intention (that's right, I am acting as the mouthpiece of God via his word) for sex to break up marriages. We have taken sex so totally out of its context that it is actually destroying families and marriages. I challenge every one of you seeking to one day marry or remarry to search your hearts and your motives for wanting to be married. Please don't marry someone if you have the wrong focus, because your marriage may fail and some people never recover from divorce. Some people with failed marriages become bitter, angry and some get so depressed that they lose their will to live and become suicidal. Yes, even some Christians have entertained suicide, because when you open yourself up to the enemy, he does what he does. "He comes to steal, kill and destroy, but Christ came that we might have life more abundantly (St. John 10:10).

Life Lessons

- Make sure you are in love and not in lust when you marry. Marriage will provide plenty of challenges, don't add to them.

- Never compare your ex-boyfriends or girlfriends to your mate; you have to allow them space to be themselves and to work on loving you as they are.

- Discuss sex before you marry. Failure to do so can cause all types of problems.

- Never isolate your mate from his/her friends they had before they married you unless it is proven that these friends are a negative influence.

- Depending on your age "love" is an emotion, so in addition to love please make sure you understand the covenant of marriage.

Situation #4

The Marriage of Convenience: Selfish Sylvia & Convenient Curtis

Selfish is defined as:

- Concerned excessively or exclusively with oneself : seeking or concentrating on one's own advantage, pleasure, or well-being without regard for others
- Arising from concern with one's own welfare or advantage in disregard of others <a *selfish* act>

Convenience is defined as:

- The state of being able to proceed with something with little effort or difficulty

Convenient is defined as:

- A quality or situation that makes something easy or useful for someone by reducing the amount of work or time required to do something
- A time that is appropriate for doing something or that is suitable for someone
- Something (such as a device) or a person that makes you more comfortable or allows you to do things more easily

Out of all the bad situations that occur in marriages, the selfish and convenient marriage appears that they should make it. With them being adults and having all types of situations in the past, we can put this marriage of convenience together and grow old together as mature adults. Look at this situation and watch what happens in a marriage of convenience when selfishness is involved.

Convenient Curtis is this fine caramel brother, right physique, easy to look at and has a good job. He comes with some physical, emotional and mental baggage that is clearly not seen. Although he is the complete outer package, his focus is solely on what's convenient for him. He's been hurt, physically and emotionally so he is Tina Turner's friend, "What's Love Got To Do With It" – "Who needs a heart when a heart can be broken?" Oh and did I mention that this man has the gift of Prophet/Preacher.

Selfish Sylvia is educated, pretty, has a body to kill for and is excellent with her finances. She has A-1 credit which is always a plus for the brothers who are looking for a woman of convenience. Good credit is a requirement for these brothers, who would not pay the dollar store what was owed and have the wrong focus. She is the perfect image of what a wife should be, minus the cooking. She's been hurt in the church, mentally abused at home by both parents, often hurt by men and is just the puppy looking for love in all the wrong places. She looks like a sweet girl, but on the inside, she is secretly selfish because of the things she's endured.

Why couldn't they make it? Two successful people, both in the church, at the top of their game in the business world, they failed because they did not have the foundation of love and mutual respect for one another. Selfish Sylvia really loved him. She endured the pain of him having multiple relationships (when they were not together, but she had hidden hopes) loving others and rejecting her. He even married another woman and when that failed, he dated another woman and wished to marry her but that did not turn out well. So after all of the mental and physical abuse he suffered, he finally turned to Sylvia. He did not look at her because he thought she was his queen or because he knew that she was his virtuous woman; he married her out of convenience for himself. After all, she watched him squeeze her heart into pieces, prefer other women above her, and she still wanted him at a time his ego needed to be wanted. He thought to himself, *after all the hell I've been through in relationships, I am going to marry her, not because I love her, but because I know that she loves me.*

Why shouldn't this marriage work if she actually loved him? Should a marriage where one person loves the other work? No, because it's one-sided and anything that is one-sided will eventually become lopsided. Lopsided things have an imbalance and imbalance will eventually wreck a marriage. Why? Because when one person loves and the other person can take the mate or leave her, she will usually be neglected and then thrown away. That's how quiet affairs begin. Quiet affairs are those affairs that begin mentally; they start in the mind and then they become emotional (no sex, just leaning on each other for emotional support). Quiet affairs start with the roaming of the eyes, the hidden desire for another, extreme vulnerability and an open heart where another woman/man can sneak in and become the focus of your attention and affection. Remember, Convenient Curtis never really loved her; she was his bride of convenience so he could have a little sex and not be alone. That's why it was so easy for him to just walk away, even though they had children together.

Christians have to remember there is a price to pay for going against the commandments of God and oh, the price he paid.

She never knew what happened. How her dream and long-awaited marriage was crumbling right in front of her face. Yes, she had some issues but they were there before they were married. Yes, she was self-centered, but she had a right to be. After all, he pursued her for his convenience. She confronted the soon-to-be mistress in an attempt to save her marriage. She told her that if he was doing this to his wife, he would do it to her also. She requested that she not pursue her husband and the mistress denied that they were having an affair even though an emotional affair had begun.

The moral of this situation is that a marriage of convenience in the Body of Christ will not work; unless the couple realizes what happened, seeks counseling and fights to make the marriage work. God ordained marriage for his purpose and not for our convenience. Marriages of convenience rarely work because when the person who sought the marriage for the convenience is not fulfilled, it's easy for the unattached heart to look elsewhere for convenience and maybe even love.

She is left to her hurt, which makes her even more selfish, because she gave and even though she was a little self-centered, she deserved better. Now she has to deal with even more abandonment, rejection and the scars of raising children without a present father. So, brothers, consider when you marry for your own selfish convenience, consider your family, the pain that you have caused someone's daughter and the ills and dysfunction that you may put on your own children. Remember, "Be not deceived, God is not mocked, for whatsoever a man soweth, that shall he/she also reap, Galatians 6:7." You just don't know how your reaping will be repaid to you.

Life Lessons

If a man always prefers other women and comes back to you when he constantly breaks up with them, look deep within yourself and see if you are the rebound girl.

Know that when a man constantly hurts you emotionally and gives you the 'so what I don't care attitude' that he will never consider you his queen; you are probably his girl of convenience.

Sometimes men don't realize what they have until they get into other relationships and then they realize that you were the one. Make him work for you; don't give him your heart so easily, protect yourself and give it some time before you jump into the emotion of love.

*Michelle McKinney Hammond, states that "Patience is the virtue that forces deception to reveal itself." Give it time and you will see if he is for real.

Work on your self-esteem and know that you are a queen and you do not have to settle for Convenient Curtis, because God has a man who will love you, for you. You Just Have to Wait!

Situation #5

Abuse - Abusive Alvin and Needy Netty

Please know that when a man beats a woman, he is really beating himself, because of the rage and disappointment he has towards himself inwardly. That statement is not biblical, psychological, or what a survey says. It is my personal view. Although I am sure if I did a study, some psychologist or survey taken would probably agree with me.

Abuse is defined as:

- to use (something) to bad effect or for a bad purpose, misuse
- treat (a person or an animal) with cruelty or violence, especially regularly or repeatedly
- speak in an insulting and offensive way to or about (someone)
- the improper use of something
- cruel and violent treatment of a person or animal.
- insulting and offensive language

Abuse comes in several forms:

Physical Abuse - Violent behavior in the form of hitting, with one's fist or items such as knives, guns, etc.

Verbal Abuse - The speaking of negative things towards a person, such as cursing, putting a person down verbally, and those devastating phrases such as, you will never be nothing, stupid, you come from nothing so nothing from nothing leaves nothing and you are nothing.

Emotional Abuse - One definition of emotional abuse is, "any act including confinement, isolation, verbal assault, humiliation, intimidation, infantilization, or any other treatment which may diminish the sense of identity, dignity, and self-worth.

*Emotional abuse is also known as psychological abuse

Needy Netty is the girl who is usually attractive on the outside but lacks self-esteem. She has gone through so much in life that she sometimes does not even think for herself, she just needs. She needs a man to tell her what to do, where to do it at and how to do it. She has usually stopped thinking for herself because she is so eager to please others and to be accepted and loved by someone, just anyone, that she does not ever consider herself in any situation.

Abusive Alvin preys on women like Needy Netty because he sees she has no self-worth. He sneaks up on her with kindness and once he gets her, the abuse begins. The first form of abuse is usually verbal and then physical. If she gets the courage to tell him that she is leaving, he'll act disappointed that she is going and promise never to do it again. He verbally conveys that he loves her and that he was just angry because of... or whatever situation he can think of to get her to stay.

Needy Netty, in most cases, can have it going on. A sister with a degree and a good job but somewhere in life, she just lost her self-worth. This usually happens when a person is told something negative in their childhood (even though she/he has climbed above the negative statement, that statement still choked their self-worth); went through a bad relationship where she was emotionally abused or just looked at her situation because she was the only one without a husband and thought, well, a piece of a man is better than no man at all. This can be a woman who loves God but because her focus is off, and she is on the "I need a man path," she finds herself in this situation. You may be saying to yourself, come on; this is not real, but you would be surprised at the amount of domestic violence that goes on in Christian marriages. If we marry men who go to church but are not totally sold out to God, we get the undelivered man. Whatever he has not dealt with, will come out in some form when we date him; we tend to overlook that fault because we do not see the whole picture while dating them.

So now Needy Netty, who just needs a man to help her find her self-worth, is in an abusive relationship. The sad thing is that sometimes because he has not started beating on her physically, she does not realize that she is being emotionally/mentally abused. It is something in the woman psyche that lets us adapt to our environment, even when it is negative. This is probably because before wickedness entered into the picture, God made Eve for the man and she was to adapt to his environment before all of this sin and calamity came into the world. Netty's girlfriends try to help her and tell her that she deserves better but she thinks, *oh, Alvin's okay; he will change.* **Alvin will never change until he gets help and acknowledges that he has a problem.**

Alvin never addresses his issues so he becomes more and more angry and takes it out on Netty. Leaders may not know it, and it will never be admitted, but there are people sitting in the church who need some psychological counselling by a professional provider. People will never admit that they may need some additional help outside of what the church offers, by a professional trained counsellor. His verbal and emotional abuse now becomes violent. Netty does not see her self-worth so she allows it. She thinks she can help him, but he is beyond help. He constantly beats her and is always sorry, until one day he beats her to death.

**<u>Women, please know that if a man beats on you, it's not love; it's rage and anger.</u>

Please get out of this type of relationship. You are worth so much more and you deserve better. If his anger is not addressed and he doesn't get some type of help, I am afraid you might become a victim of death. I have personally seen this with a friend who was killed by a violently raging man who was supposed to have loved her.

Brothers, if violence is a part of your life and you for some reason find yourself always angry enough to want to hit a woman, please seek help. If you don't address the anger in violence within you, you may find yourself getting help via the prison system. This type of punishment affects not only the woman you are beating on but will have a profound effect on your children and family members. Imagine the hardship that you put on your family when you are not there to provide for them physically, emotionally and financially.

Life Lessons

Violence is not an indication of love. If he beats you, he has no regard for you.

You are worth much more then you think. If you think you have to take what is dished out to you and it is all negative, please get some counseling before he kills you.

Men, if you beat on women, you should take some self-esteem and anger classes, because you are not really angry at your target, but you are angry at yourself and have inner struggles going on.

Personal Counseling is not a sign of weakness but an indication that you are aware there is a problem somewhere, and you have to get to the source in order to be made whole.

Do not yoke yourself up with a mate if you know you have unresolved issues, rage and financial problems.

Another Marriage Situation

Although this marriage did not end in divorce, I feel the need to share this story. This situation should make both men and women look at the choices they make when selecting a mate. (I Samuel 25:1-42). I will give you a short overview of the characters and the moral of the story.

I Samuel 25 introduces us to three main characters, David, Nabal and Abigail.

David, a man after God's own heart, was anointed as a child to be king over Israel.

Nabal was a wealthy, ignorant, selfish and foolish man, who was the husband of Abigail.

Abigail was a beautiful, intelligent, wise woman who was married to Nabal, the fool.

Please read the full story when you get a chance, but I will abbreviate what happened. David moved to a new location after Samuel the prophet died. The place where he settled was near Nabal's property and business in the field. While David was there, he acted as a man of nobility, looked out for Nabal's men in the form of a protector, and did not steal or take anything when he had the opportunity to do so. In other words, David acted as man of integrity.

One day during the time of shearers (where they cut the lamb's wool) Nabal had a little gathering. Since David was fair to Nabal's servants, he sent word to Nabal by his young men, who greeted Nabal honorably. David sent word and asked Nabal to send them a little something during his festivity. In layman's terms, David asked him to send a couple of platters, basically share some of his food with them because they knew he had plenty. David figured that since he was fair to Nabal and his men that at this time, he would not mind sharing with them. Nabal, being the harsh, foolish, ass that he was, instead of just saying no, he hurled insults at David. Why should I share with you, Jesse's boy? This is the stuff I have worked for and labored to get. He stated, 'I understand that servants are running away from their masters every day,' insinuating David's situation with Saul. (I am paraphrasing to bring the language up to today's terminology), but do I look like the government or the welfare system? So he did not share his goods with David.

David's young men came back and stated to David everything that Nabal said. David, in his fury, told the men to suit up, they were going to war. "Since he was so disrespectful, we are going to kill him and all of his men."

Meanwhile, one of Nabal's servants slid up to Abigail and told her, "You know, your husband was quite rude to David's young men. While we were taking care of business, David and his men looked out for us. They did not steal anything and they made sure that no one else stole from us, either. All they asked for was just a little leftovers and your husband just went off. We'd better hope that David doesn't confront Nabal and cause bloodshed."

Now this is the moral of the story… Abigail and her wise self looked out for her husband in the absence of his sanity. Although man is our covering, Abigail had to cover her husband in his foolishness **(women, our jobs are never done)**. She prepared food and told the men to go before her and take David and his men some food and she would meet them later. Later, she went to greet David and basically smooth things over. She advised him that he was a man of God and he didn't want blood shed on his hands, not even the blood of a fool. She calmed David down and made him see the error of his way. He, in his own way, repented and thanked Abigail. Later, Nabal died and David remembered Abigail and sent for her. So she now went from being married to an ass, to her God-given king.

IN A Nutshell

Be careful that you don't yoke yourself up with a fool even if he has money.

Know that there will be times when you have to look out for your husband beyond your quote, unquote "duty".

Women, we have to understand that even though God has called man to be our covering, we may have to cover their foolishness in certain situations. We are their helpmates.

Women, again, we have to make sure we stop looking at the outer appearance when choosing to be found by a man, because money is not everything; ask Abigail.

Men, understand that your woman is your help; you may be getting ready to make a mistake that is detrimental to your future, but if you would just listen to her, you could avoid a major catastrophe.

For Women Only – <u>To Thine Own Self Be True</u>

In the last marital situation, I wrote about Abigail and Nabal. Abigail was pretty, educated and wise beyond her tradition. Nabal had money, but his very name meant fool or foolish one. The *scripture* does not tell us how they ended up together, so I will be the voice of our current society. Do you think Abigail married him because he could cause her to live on easy street and shop on Rodeo Drive? What about the status that comes with being married to a wealthy man? Women, we have to be true to ourselves, so this is for you.

For Women Only

Nabal's very name means foolish/folly. Before you married your mate, did you see some sign(s) that there would be problems because of his activity? What were they?

_____
_____
_____
_____
_____

The truth be told, I should not have married him because:

_____
_____
_____
_____
_____
_____

I was selfish and I married him because:

_____
_____
_____
_____
_____
_____

If I had the chance to do it again, I would change:

_____
_____
_____
_____
_____
_____
_____
_____

The next time I get married, I will:

_____
_____
_____
_____

Since I am being true to myself, I must take my part in the failed marriage because I:

_____
_____
_____
_____
_____
_____
_____
_____
_____

I can truly say that I did or did not do everything to save my marriage:
Think about it truthfully.

_____
_____
_____
_____
_____

Since I have not made peace with my failed marriage, I will reach out to my husband and apologize if necessary or tell him how I feel:

_____

_____

_____

_____

_____

_____

_____

_____

_____

I want to be free from my pain or disappointment so as my personal therapy, I must note what I am really feeling:

_____

_____

_____

_____

_____

Have I really forgiven my mate for what happened in our marriage? If I haven't, I must:

_____
_____
_____
_____
_____
_____

My standard for my next marriage if I remarry will be:

_____
_____
_____
_____
_____
_____
_____
_____
_____

In addition, I must deal with my emotions because:

_____
_____
_____
_____
_____
_____
_____
_____
_____
_____
_____
_____
_____
_____
_____
_____
_____
_____
_____
_____
_____

Notes for Your Thoughts

Chapter IX
Abandonment – Should I Stay

So it's not gonna be easy. It's going to be really hard; we're gonna have to work at this every day, but I want to do that because I want you. I want all of you, forever, every day. You and me... every day."
— <u>Nicholas Sparks</u>, <u>The Notebook</u>

Do Not Become Bitter
Become Better

Should I Stay?

After all of the hurt and emotions that we go through (everyone's emotions are different) we have to ask ourselves, "should I stay?" One of the hardest questions that you will have to ask yourself as a Christian, is this, "should I stay?" The songwriter said, "I have had some good days and I have had some hills to climb, I asked the question, Lord, why so much pain?" The writer goes on to say, "But he knows what's best for me even though my weary eyes can't see, <u>so I will just say thank you, Lord, and I won't complain.</u>" After you have stood up in church with your spiritual self and basically said everything you were taught to say, you have quoted all of the spiritual clichés (God is good, all the time, and all the time, God is good; Praise the Lord, He is worthy to be praised) you have to go somewhere and deal with your emotions. We fight through the spiritual aspect of the matter, because we were taught strongly and without excuse that God does not like divorce. The Bible says so (St Mark 10:39). So now I have a dilemma to deal with because when they questioned Jesus about divorces or putting your spouse away, he said, "From the beginning of time, it (divorce) was not to be, but because of the hardening of your hearts, it was allowed."

So now the battle begins in the mind. Am I going against the word of the God? So while I am fighting and struggling in my mind, I have to take a long look at the marriage. I have to weigh the good and the bad and come up with a solution. If you've looked in your heart and find that you want to stay and your mate agrees to work <u>with you</u>, you should definitely stay and work it out. Marriage is hard work and it costs a lot on both parties' part, so I encourage you to leave the past behind and to work on your future of getting to a healthy and happy marriage.

On the other hand, if you recognize that after weighing things, you are in a bad situation, you should probably go. If you find that you are getting the short end of the deal and your mate has no compromise in him/her, it's probably better that you go. Personally and biblically, getting the short end of the deal is no reason to leave a marriage, but what can you do when you've yoked yourself up with an ass? After you've prayed, dealt with your emotions, searched the scriptures, found out what love was according to Corinthians the love chapter, realized what marriage is and what a Christian man and woman should do and be, per Paul's writings in Corinthians and Ephesians, if you can't come up with a resolution to make your marriage work, I say you should go. (Again, this is my personal view based on my own personal experience. Please view the notes and consider your individual situation. I definitely encourage you to work it out if your marriage can be saved.) When you get to the judgmental folks, you can simply say, "What God has joined together, let no man put asunder." Now the question is did God join us together? There are a whole lot of questions that will be asked and you have to make up in your mind that you only owe God an explanation and not man.

When your marriage is over, you have to look in your heart and in the mirror and realize that it is over. Staying in a dead-end marriage with a person who doesn't want a divorce but doesn't want to work on the marriage, will only <u>paralyze your life.</u> Yes, you will become stagnated and stuck. Simply wasting time and letting years of your life pass you by, and for what? You should go for your own mental stability. Realize that staying in a fruitless marriage will eventually play on your psyche and eventually cause you to lose your self-esteem.

Should I Stay – Continued

She-Motions

The pain of a decision to let your marriage go and sever ties has to be called, She-Motions. Only she can tell you of the emotions that she feels about a crumbling marriage. Every woman handles their emotions differently. I don't believe there is one woman who would say that the break-up of her marriage was not very emotional. You gave your heart, your body, and your dreams to him. You entrusted him to be the priest over you and your house, and in most cases, he has failed you miserably.

How do you get through this without killing him, verbally or physically? Remember, no matter how hurt or disappointed we are at our mates, we are still Christians and "Thou Shall Not Kill." So you cannot assassinate him with your mouth or in any other manner. Although you may have a reason, but you don't have a right. When we choose to follow God's way, it is spiritual and then emotional. We grew up with all of these rules and regulations about marriage and divorce in the church. We were told that Christians should never divorce, no matter what the situation is. Then the men who were married to us, who liked men, came out of the closet. You know the brothers on the down low, and the church was not prepared for this. Then the men who liked to beat on women became bold with their violence, then tried to spiritualize it by misinterpreting the scriptures, were exposed and we were not prepared to deal with this either in the church. Let us not forget the men who liked little girls and little boys. We were just telling people what we thought because we were not inside the situation. Yes, there are women who married men, who liked women, and all sorts of craziness is going on. A woman burning in her lust, preferring a sex toy instead of a man; this all goes against the nature of God, but I will mention this because I don't want you to think I am being one-sided.

(But remember this book is from a woman's point of view.)

So now we are forced to deal with **"Situations"** and no one knows what to do. The church doesn't want everyone doing what they think is right in their own eyes (nor does God) so we have a dilemma. How do we handle divorce in the church? Should a person be able to get out of a marriage when they've married a man who likes little boys and little girls? What about the woman who is being beaten constantly and is a nervous wreck because she doesn't know if the next blow is going to send her to glory prematurely. I am going to tell you to get out of this marriage. Search the scriptures and seek God for yourself, because it is your emotions that are being bounced on, and in the end, you are ultimately the person who is going to pay for staying. Regardless, if it's physically (the consequences of being beaten), emotionally (with bad nerve constantly living in fear), or spiritually (so bogged down with the strongholds in your life that you can't praise God), you will be the one who ultimately pays for staying in an abusive marriage. Divorce is situational, not personal. I believe that's why God's word says in Hebrews 13:4, "Whoremongers and Adulterers, he would judge," because he knows that you are judging from what appears to be, but he knows all.

So now the marriage is dissolved and you have to deal with your emotions and the judgment of others. The pain and the judgment of others is almost equivalent to the emotional pain of the death of your marriage. Where do people get off putting their two cents in your business? How can they pass judgment on you? They were not there to hear what he said to you or how he treated you. They were not there when the covenant took place during the engagement and then the wedding, so how can they speak on it? No one knows what goes on inside a marriage but the people in it and God. They may tell others things and people judge you based on what was said, but remember, believe half of what you hear and even less of what you see.

"The Great Façade" lives in most marriages and especially when they begin to crumble. If immaturity lives in the marriage – wow, you get to see some of the ugliest things you could ever imagine in a Christian marriage. The strongest thing a woman feels in her emotions is abandonment. A turmoil of she-motions comes with this feeling, not necessarily because he left the premises, but because he broke all of the promises and failed her. He left her emotionally, to deal with the things he promised but never delivered, the shattered dreams of being one forever, while he realized he needed time to grow up and handle things differently. So she deals with the fact that her time and money were wasted on a wedding, a honeymoon and all of the bliss that came with his promises. This is definitely one-sided, but read the next page for <u>Men Only</u> and you will understand why she gets to make this one-sided statement as she deals with the situation alone.

These Pages are for Men Only

But I would have you to know.
that the head of every man is Christ
And the head of the woman is man (I Corinthians 11:3 in part)

When we married you, we gave you what we had to give and you were supposed to cover us. Men, please know that God has made you the head of the house, and as such, you are responsible to cover your wife, financially, emotionally and spiritually. If you find that you cannot cover a woman, do not marry her. You may think that this is one-sided, but we have to come out of this worldly way of thinking about marriage. It was not a woman's choice that you would be the head of her, it was God's choice. Personally, if I could change things around, I would make a woman to be a man's covering because as women, we are being failed on every hand. However, because we follow God, you are the head of us and even when we marry you and we fail you in situations, (we may have confided some personal things to a friend who turned everything we said around to disappoint you, we may have spoken out of turn, we may even have been disrespectful to you, but it is your job to put things in order). No Godly woman ever marries a man with the intentions of saying, "Oh, I am going to marry him, hurt him or disrespect him. This is "situational" stuff, and as the head of the house, you have to be mature enough to sit your wife down and fix things. Yes, you are the fixer as the head of the house and the head of the woman. Women also have a part to play in trying to make the marriage work, but God ultimately made man the head, so like it or not, the responsibility falls on you as the head. Remember, "Failure is an Excuse -Success is a Choice- that comes with hard work and prayer." (Understand that there are some situations a man cannot control, such as a woman who just doesn't want to be married to him any longer. But he still has to search to see if her desire to not be a part of his life is a result of something that he has done. Men, you have to get out of this thinking that the woman God gave you, gave you of the fruit to eat and you were deceived because of the woman. O man thou are inexcusable! Read Genesis 3:1-24. "The Fall of Man" because you are inexcusable, the fact that you elected to eat the fruit does not excuse you of your responsibility and the part that you played in the fall. Adam, where art thou? You can no longer hide yourself. The consequence of sin has caused you some things, but it did not cause you your position as the head of the woman. Enough with the excuses, get back in your place, because if you fail to cover us, you will be held liable and accountable to God, not to mention the mess that you are making on the earth. Again, if you cannot cover a woman financially, spiritually and emotionally, do not marry her. It is your responsibility to be the head, simply because that is the way God wanted it to be. Oh, men of God, you can no longer view her lips, hips and fingertips, because your responsibility to her goes much deeper than the fulfilling of your flesh. Confess to yourself, you married her because she looked good and you wanted to roll in the sack with her for your own selfish pleasure. You failed to see that marriage is so much deeper than that and what you thought. Mistakes are made, but how many times will you marry before you realize the problem is you? Please consider who you are and where God has placed you, because just like He will not change his position on where He has placed you as the head, He will not go back on his word. Galatians 6:7 tells us to "Be not deceived, God is not mocked, for whatsoever a man soweth that shall he also reap." I am going to give you some lines on this page to deal with the women you have hurt because of the mistakes you have made just because you wanted some sex and some temporary companionship.

My Notes for Men Only

If the truth be told, I could have avoided my divorce if I would have:_____

_____

_____

_____

_____

_____

_____

I can now admit to myself the truth, and that is that I should not have married her because:

_____

_____

_____

_____

_____

_____

_____

I take responsibility for my failed marriage and I will contact her and apologize because God made me the head and I failed her for whatever reason...

_____

_____

_____

_____

_____

_____

_____

_____

I must deal with:

_____

_____

_____

_____

_____

_____

Now back to her emotions. When failed marriages cause the emotion of bitterness, please go to the altar and cry out to God. When you become bitter, you stop producing, and when you stop producing, your life is unproductive and you become stagnant and die, even though you are walking among the living. You can't grow because you have let the bitterness of life and an unforgiving spirit enter your heart. Hebrew 12:14-15, tells us to make every effort to live peaceful with all men and to be holy; without holiness, no one will see the Lord. It admonishes us to see that no one misses the grace of God and that no bitter root grows up to cause trouble and defile many. You see the root of bitterness can be towards someone. That someone is usually a person who has hurt you, like an ex-husband or wife, or someone you trusted in authority. Shake it off, the root of bitterness. It can destroy you, and in the end, the person is not even worth it.

Bishop Jakes wrote a book called "LET IT GO" and I encourage you to purchase it. He gives some facts about un-forgiveness and I quote him verbatim from his book:

- ❖ Un-forgiveness comes when we believe that our future has been taken from us or irreparably damaged

- ❖ Un-forgiveness comes when we believe that betrayal has not been sufficiently atoned

- ❖ Un-forgiveness comes as a defense mode to protect the bruised inner self which often is hidden from view or even our own awareness

- ❖ Un-forgiveness comes when we feel we have been deceived in some way or publicly humiliated

- ❖ Un-forgiveness comes when personal trust has been violated

- ❖ Un-forgiveness comes from opportunities lost

- ❖ Un-forgiveness comes when we have been forced to suffer the soul wounds of abuse, neglect and rejection in silence

Wow, are these some deep and true statements. I believe that these un-forgiveness statements can also apply to the root of bitterness. Un-forgiveness and the root of bitterness can cause you to miss out on so many things because you hold the hurt. Let it go. The funny thing is that the people who have hurt us have moved on with their lives and have become very productive in life. "Let Go Of The Hurt" that causes you to be bitter, unforgiving and unproductive because, in the end, you will only hurt yourself more. Even if your ex-spouse may have hurt you but can't man up and be mature enough to apologize, forgive him or her anyway. You will be stronger, wiser and better once you look at the man/woman in the mirror. As emotional as we are, because that's how God made us as women, we are not to let our emotions drive us. We must admit through the turmoil of divorce our emotions are very noisy for a few simple reasons:

- It wasn't supposed to happen to me.
- What will people think?
- What about my position in the church?
- What I taught against now applies to me.
- How can I hold my head up and teach people to work through their marriages when my marriage failed?
- I must go back to practicing abstinence from sex.
- I am losing my financial help, so now I may have to struggle.

Even through the struggle of our noisy emotions, we must not let them control us. If you let your emotions control you, you will end up lost, without direction and on the wrong side of your destiny.

Since your marriage has failed, it is dead, bury it. Stop looking at what should have been because it did not happen the way you planned. When you bury that failed marriage, bury the hurt and disappointment it has caused you. Move on with your life. God will turn your pain into a blessing and qualify you to walk others through "The Pain of Divorce."

Notes for Your Thoughts

Chapter X

Gullible Girls and Belligerent Bad Boys

Hope deferred maketh the heart sick. (Proverbs 13:12)

Art thou he that should come or look we for another? (Luke 7:19)

This know also, that in the last days perilous times shall come. For men shall be lovers of their own selves, covetous, boasters, proud, blasphemers, disobedient to parents, unthankful, unholy, without natural affection, trucebreakers, false accusers, incontinent, fierce, despisers of those that are good, traitors, heady, high-minded, lovers of pleasures more than lovers of God. (II Timothy 3:1-4)

I started this chapter segment with these scripture references because the Bible states that there is nothing new under the sun. So I feel the need to address John's question, my version for the purpose of this chapter. Are you the Christ or should we look for another? John was the preparer of the way for Jesus. After he did everything that was right according to the scripture and prophesy, he ended up in an unsure state of mind. So he sent his disciples to question Jesus about his position. 'Are you the Messiah or should we expect someone else?' In our times of waiting, our faith is tested.

Hope deferred makes the heart sick, deals with our emotion of waiting. We've prayed, fasted and done everything that Momma and the leaders of the church told us to do, yet we find ourselves in the state of singleness, not married. We have to watch that emotion because the enemy of our soul can and will present doubt in our minds. The scripture states, Hebrews 11:1 that **Now Faith** is the substance of things hoped for and the evidence of things not seen. If we do not watch ourselves and stay grounded in the Word, we will start looking at the here and now. We have to watch this state of mind because the just shall live by his/her faith. Focusing on what we see produces Gullible Girls.

The definition of gullible is: Easily deceived or duped or easily fooled or cheated.

So often because we wait as singles and stand up for Christ (via our practice of abstinence from sex) and our lifestyle, we start wondering where is my Prince Charming? Nature is calling and that empty bed is not very appealing to us. Young Woman's Christian Council and the Church Mothers taught us to pray and God would send us someone, that special anointed man of God who would treat us so well. So when the circumstances of our single life hit us and we are tired of waiting, we question ourselves and God. Hope deferred causes gullible girls to look in the face of all his faults, failures and excuses and try to make the frog a prince. If he is a frog, we can't kiss him and make him a prince, sorry, that is a fairytale.

Men who have froglike symptoms and tendencies will never be your prince. Frogs hop from place to place, because it's in their nature. They don't have to stay in one place. So a man who hops from woman to woman or wife to wife is not qualified to be your prince, because he has no stability. In most cases, not all, these are men who prey on women who have their own things. These women usually have their own homes, cars, bank accounts etc.. These men go from woman to woman, they marry multiple wives because once she realizes that she kissed a frog who can't become a prince, she has to deal with her poor choice of being found by the wrong man. In most instances when she tries to address his froglike tendencies, she gets to see the bad boy's belligerence. They are angry at themselves because they knew they were frogs and when she addresses it, their immaturity comes out which usually causes a blow out and she has to throw him back in the pond. It is usually not her will to throw him back in the pond but remember, everything is situational.

Belligerent Bad Boys, these are the boys who appear to have it together. They look the part but they can't separate lies, untruths or dreams from reality, and they lack integrity. An evangelist said to me, "Do you know the difference between honesty and integrity?" My statement was, "Of course, I do." He proceeded to share an incident with me so I will share it with you. There was a man who went to Burger King to get something to eat. He paid for the food and the lady gave him the food in the bag. When he got to the car, he noticed that instead of his food being in the bag, it was a bag full of money. He said, "I can't keep this money." He took the money back to the store and the manager thanked him and told him that they had so many robberies that they decided to put the money in bags. The young lady who waited on him was not aware of that so she probably did not realize that she gave him the money bag.

The manager said, "You were so nice and honest, we are going to call one of the TV channels and have them do a story on your honesty because someone else would have taken the money. The man replied, "Please don't do that because my girlfriend doesn't know that I have a wife." He was an honest man with no integrity.

- Gullible Girls: if he doesn't have good work ethics before he marries you, the chances that he will work and keep a steady job after he marries you are slim to none. Pay Attention:

- If he doesn't pay his bills or bills period before he marries you, I can assure you that he will not pay the bills once you marry him.
- If he is a slob before he marries you, I can assure that he will not clean up his mess after he marries you. (If you have a problem cleaning behind him or being the maid, you might not want to marry this type of man).
- If he is violent and mean before he marries you, get ready for the fight after the honeymoon because the violence and anger in him cannot change without a change. Anger unaddressed will continue and even though you think you are not the one, you will be subject to physical and mental beat downs.
- If he has no respect for you before he marries you, don't be appalled that he has no respect for you after he marries you.

All of the above are froglike tendencies. Don't kiss the frog in hopes that he will turn into a prince, sorry to cancel the fantasy; he will not turn into a prince.

We were at a fellowship just talking about marriages and relationships in the church world because one of our mutual friends was about to end his third marriage, and before the marriage had ended, he had his eye on the fourth wife prospect. So, of course, we started conversing about what happens before, during and after relationships and people's lack of commitment when one of my friends said, "I teach my daughter if a man really wants you, he will do what you require." He told his daughter if she wants all of her M&M candies to be yellow, if the man really wants her or cares for her, he will pick through all of the candies just to get the yellow ones for her. Ladies, while I agree that this is true, if a man really wants you, he will go out of his way to give you what you want, just make sure it is genuine. Frogs can play the game and temporarily give you what you want just to get in a relationship with you, and once they are in, they show you all of their froggish ways. Please don't marry them, throw them back into the pond. Remember, patience is the virtue that forces deception to reveal itself.

It is amazing how good girls are always attracted to bad boys. Yes, even in the church. The only difference is that the bad boys in the church are not the ones who steal things from the store, or break in people's houses, rape girls or abuse little boys and intentionally destroy everything around them. The bad boys in the church are the men who are lovers of themselves more than lovers of God. If a man loves his desires and his ways more than the things of God, he is destined to break your heart. (We must know that certainly if a man or a woman, in this case, chooses to please himself/herself and does not choose to follow the will of God or do the things that please God, the lust of the flesh is about to take over and destroy the relationship <u>definitely a frog</u>).

The funny thing is that frogs, the bad boys in the church in most cases, will do what they have to do to get you but nothing to keep you. This is their inability to communicate what they want after they feel that they have made the attempt to give you what you want. It's amazing in relationships how everyone states that they are these great communicators but have the inability to convey what they feel. This causes all types of problems because when your magical mind can't translate or comprehend what they are thinking, the bad boys become belligerent. Belligerent is defined as hostile or aggressive, feeling ready to fight. So you can imagine the environment that the lack of communication creates.

Although the church bad boys do not have the characteristics stated above, they steal in the worst way, because in their belligerence, they will try to steal your joy and diminish your self-worth and self-esteem. When they are not financially capable, they will try to squeeze your finances and when you make them stand up, be a man and take responsibility, you will see all hell break loose, totally unnecessarily. You will see a grown man throwing the little boy tantrum. This is the immature side of the belligerent bad boy and when he can't have his way, he puts the gullible girl in a very bad position. This is how and why Christian marriages are failing in the church, totally unnecessarily.

Gullible Girls, remember no matter what mistakes you have made in the past or the bad choices you have selected in a relationship, you should always learn from your experiences and mistakes. Learning from your mistakes will help you not to repeat them. The mistakes will also help you to address your issues and the hurt that was inflicted upon you, or the hurt that you have inflicted upon someone. You cannot afford to be bitter or wounded for life because you were deceived by a man that you thought was a man of God. Remember,

God is still working on all of us, including you. Hindsight is the worst eyesight that you can or will ever have. Hindsight should make you take your responsibility in your failed marriage or relationship. The truth be told you saw some of those froglike tendencies but you thought because you addressed what you thought were issues and he made promises, you would have the perfect marriage. Sorry, we are living in the last days and we can't always take people's word and trust what they say because they still have hidden issues. So in your next relationship/marriage pray extra hard, pay attention and remember God's word; 2 Timothy 3:1-7

But mark this: There will be terrible times in the last days. (2) People will be lovers of themselves, lovers of money, boastful, proud, abusive, disobedient to their parents, ungrateful, unholy, (3) without love, unforgiving, slanderous, without self-control, brutal, not lovers of the good, (4) treacherous, rash, conceited, lovers of pleasure rather than lovers of God—(5) having a form of godliness but denying its power. Have nothing to do with them. (6) They are the kind who worm their way into homes and gain control over weak-willed women, who are loaded down with sins and are swayed by all kinds of evil desires, (7) always learning but never able to acknowledge the truth. Gullible Girl, learn from your mistakes.

Am I a Gullible Girl? My thoughts on Gullible Girls

_____
_____
_____
_____
_____
_____
_____
_____
_____
_____
_____
_____
_____
_____
_____
_____
_____
_____
_____
_____
_____
_____
_____

Notes for Your Thoughts

Gullible Girls
Pay Attention to the Red Flags

If a man professes to be religious and has more than two wives living at one time and is pursuing you, seeking yet another wife, that's a red flag. Pay attention to the warning signs. He, in most cases, has an inability to stay committed or will run at the first sight of conflict or disagreement.

Granted, divorce is situational, but when religious men have multiple wives still living, make sure he has resolved his previous marriage issues and fixed things with his ex-wives. If not, we have to remember the

Word. The Bible is still right; you will reap what you have sown, his reaping will definitely affect you.

If a man is a certain age above 40-45 years of age (has no drug addiction or physical disabilities) has not accomplished anything, lives from place to place, has no money in the bank or access to monies via a 401k (because he has not stayed at a job long enough to obtain one) then you are most likely getting ready to marry a financially unstable person who will always want to use what you have to cover him financially. In addition, he will not have any monies put aside to cover you when you grow old.

If a man does not take care of his children, that's a sign that he lacks care and realization of his responsibility. Don't plan a family with him because he may not take care of your child, either. Understand that taking care of a child requires financial and emotional investment in a child's life.

Hindsight is the worst eye sight. It is the one sight that will not kill you, but oh, the pain it causes when you ignore what you see.

Never, never assume that because a person is called of God that they don't lack integrity or have it all together. It may not be the best thing to trust a person based on their position. Remember, gifts and callings come without repentance.

A reminder: Frogs will never turn into princes, so don't kiss them, it's a fairytale.

Notes for Your Thoughts

Chapter XI

The Death of a Marriage
Moving Forward After Divorce

It's Over
Bury It and Move On

"To Look Around Is To Be Distressed

To Look Within Is To Be Depressed

To Look Up Is To Be Blessed"

Author, Millie Stamm

Women's Devotional Bible- Classic Edition

Zondervan Bible – Page 161,

Strength for the Wilderness

THE DIVORCE POEM

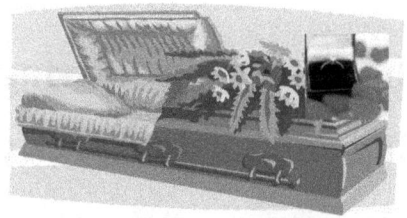

THE DEATH OF A MARRIAGE

HE PROMISED TO LOVE HONOR AND CHERISH ME
I WAS SO BLINDED, BECAUSE I TRUSTED HIM TO BE A MAN OF GOD, I JUST COULDN'T SEE

THE LACK OF INTEGRITY, HIS PROMISES MEANT NOTHING
I THOUGHT HE WAS A GOOD GUY, HIS PRAISES I WOULD SING

ONLY TO FIND OUT THAT HE WAS SO DEEP AND DARK THAT HE SANK DEEPER IN
IT WAS LIKE BEING IN THE LION'S DEN

HIS FINANCES WERE A MESS, HIS PLANS THERE WERE NONE
HE WAS JUST IRRESPONSIBLE AND WANTED TO HAVE FELLOWSHIP AND FUN

HE WAS ANGRY AT ME FOR WHAT HE DIDN'T DO
IT WAS THEN THAT I REALIZED, THIS MAN DOESN'T HAVE A CLUE

HE WANTED ME TO PAY FOR HIS PAST MISTAKES
WHO DOES THAT? BOY, GROW UP, FOR GOODNESS SAKE

I TOLD YOU WHO I WAS BEFORE I MARRIED YOU
IT'S EVIDENT THAT HE DIDN'T LISTEN, HE JUST WANTED ME TO SAY I DO

I THOUGHT HE WANTED A HELP MATE, THAT WAS JUST A JOKE
MY SUGGESTIONS WERE IGNORED AS IF THERE WERE NONE
ALWAYS THROWING TANTRUMS, I COULDN'T TAKE IT ANYMORE, I WAS DONE

WE WENT BACK AND FORTH, I TRIED TO HELP HIM GROW UP
GOD IS THIS YOUR WILL? I CAN'T DRINK FROM THIS CUP

I FEEL ABANDONED, TIME AND MONEY WASTED
TO FEED HIS EGO, I TOLERATED THAT JUNK
THE TANTRUMS, THE THREATS, LEAVING AND ACTING LIKE A PUNK

BECAUSE HE DIDN'T HANDLE THINGS PROPERLY, HE ALWAYS HAD LACK
I GAVE HIM LOVE AND MONEY TO PROVE I HAD HIS BACK

HE SAID HE WAS A COMMUNICATOR, BUT HE DID NOT TALK
ON MY FIRST ANNIVERSARY ALL ALONE I HAD TO TAKE A WALK

I CAME BACK TO DEAL WITH THE PROBLEMS WE HAD
ONLY TO GO THROUGH MORE DRAMA AND TO BE MADE SAD

HE THREW THE FINAL TANTRUM THAT BROKE THE CAMEL'S BACK
WE WERE NOW SEPARATING AND THAT WAS A FACT

NO PLANS OF RECONCILIATION, HE THOUGHT I WOULD STAY
I WAS FED UP AN NO MORE GAMES WOULD I PLAY

YOU GO YOUR WAY AND I WILL TOO
BECAUSE IT'S EVIDENT, THAT I AM NO LONGER YOUR BOO

I WILL DEAL WITH THE MISTAKE THAT I HAVE MADE
AND THE CONSEQUENCES THAT THROUGH THIS BAD CHOICE, MUST BE PAID

IN MY GOD I WILL TRUST AND ALWAYS REJOICE
THIS MARRIAGE IS OVER AND WILL END IN DIVORCE

Although ending a marriage can be devastating to both parties, it is sometimes needed. I question all people who stand on their convictions that divorce should never occur amongst the Saints/Christians. Should one stay in a marriage of misery? As previously stated, the Bible declares that whoremongers and adulterers, God will judge. Have you ever wondered why? There are some situations that you will never see nor would you ever believe that occur in marriages before the divorce takes place. You will never know how, although they have been hurt by each other, how mates sometimes still protect each other and their reputations. Could you imagine if everything, every little detail, was disclosed that happens in a leader's marriage that has failed? That would have a devastating effect on the believers as well as the unbelievers.

Could you imagine the pastor's wife entering the sanctuary and when he gets up to proclaim God's Word, she stands up and says the message for today is that your pastor likes little boys, or better yet, he has slept with more than 25 percent of the woman in this church, while married to me? How would you like to know that while your pastor can preach you under the bench, he is mean and beats on his wife? Before you wonder to yourself, how anointed a man of God could be if he does all of these things, remember that "the gifts and callings of God are without repentance" – Romans 11:29), so we are not the ones who can judge them. God gave them a gift and despite the fact that they may not be good relational, they are the ones God selected to proclaim the gospel. I am not one-sided when it comes to this, there are also situations that men have to deal with, such as wives having affairs with men in the church. How would you like to hear the pastor come out and say, oh pray for me because I just caught my wife in bed with another woman? Better yet, I came home to find out that she packed up all of the furniture, emptied the bank account and is now living with her boy toy. Oh no, that can't be, oh yes, the devil is loose and he is wreaking havoc on our marriages.

That is enough of those situations. I just thought I would give you some life situations to make you understand why sometimes it is better to bury the marriage and move on with your life. There are many other reasons why we must quit. Unfortunately, we cannot tell a person in similar situations what we feel until we've walked a mile in their shoes or marriage situations. Well, like it or not, we have to move on after the death of a marriage. Holding on to it will not do anyone any good. It won't help those who are in the relationship, those who are watching it, or those who are affected by it, (our children, friends, family members etc.). As stated previously, move on, don't hold the hurt because it will affect you in many ways. We still have to talk about "holding the hurt" in this chapter because as long as you hold it, you will never bury your marriage or the pain it caused you. So many people hold on to the hurt their mates have caused them that they never get to move on with their lives. If you hold the hurt, where will it take you? How will it help you and how will you ever grow into what your experiences have taught you? Let it go!

You may say to yourself, yeah, but you don't know what he/she did:
- They cheated on me
- They gave me a disease
- They lied to me and on me
- They failed to keep their part of the deal
- They mentally and physically abused me
- They were gay and married me

- They made me lose my possessions and gave me bad credit
- They hindered me in the ministry and did not want me to do anything

The list could go on and on. I hate to hear people say just move on with your life, but as harsh as that might sound, there comes a time when you just have to move on. Don't let the hurt put you in bondage and cause you to miss God and what he can do in and through you. Holding on to a bad marriage will cause you to hate and if you regard iniquity in your heart, God will not hear you. While you hate that mate he/she has remarried, switched careers, had more children and has totally moved on and you are not even a thought in his/her mind.

I encourage you to know that the marriage is dead, it is over. You may need to grieve, you may need counseling and you may even need to face your mate. But at any cost, deal with it so you can move on with your life. If your mate is not spiritual or mature enough for you to verbally speak with and address your issues, send him or her a letter, they don't have to respond, but it's off you. You have now dealt with your issue.

This advice is coming from a divorced lady who refused to hold the hurt or let her life be stunted because of a failed marriage. To make sure she was free from the hurt, she emailed her ex-husband an exit review. In the review, she stated things that occurred in their marriage and told him how she felt and encouraged him not marry another person until he deals with his issues and his inability to be truthful about matters. Laugh if you must, but that young lady is free mentally, spiritually and financially and has no illness on her because of this failed marriage.

We must learn from our mistakes and try to help our sisters and brothers avoid the same pitfalls we have experienced. Move on with your life and take a page from Brother Marvin Sapp's song, "I never would have made it without God." I recognize, because of my situation with this dead marriage, I'm Stronger, I'm Wiser and "I'm Better." You know our old sayings, "Momma said if it doesn't kill you it will make you stronger."

Put the marriage in a coffin, throw some dirt on it, bury it and go to praising God because he brought you through it with your sanity. Now turn your pain and disappointment into Ministry and confess "TO GOD BE THE GLORY FOR THE THINGS HE HAS DONE!'

The end of the Marriage and Story
The beginning of your Life

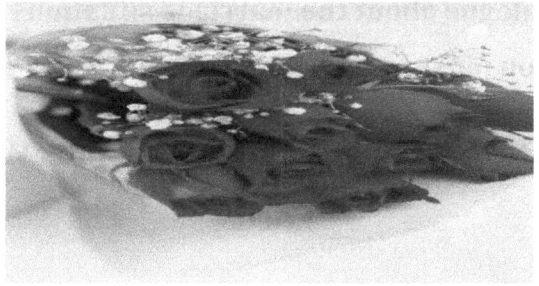

"Just know that Failure is an Excuse
and Success is a Choice"
Choose to succeed beyond the pain of your Divorce

I speak Blessings, Good Health,
Wealth and a Happy Life Over You.

Social Gatherings - Group Discussion:

Let's dialogue about the marriage situations in this book. You must be open and truthful.

Situation #1 Lust & Loving Lucious Wrong Focus

Sexual desire is a large part of why people marry. Do you think that for people of faith, the main focus for marriage is sex? Why or Why not?

Do you believe that Christians are actually abstaining from sex?

Do you think that most Christian marriages fail because we marry with the wrong focus?

In your own words, what is sexual lust?

What happens if lust is not dealt with before a couple is married?

Should Christians marry just because a baby is conceived before marriage? Why or why not?

Situation #2 Lies, Lies and Alibis

Should you look for signs while dating to check your future mate's character?

What are some of the signs you should look for?

How often should you forgive or turn your head to your **FUTURE** mate's lies?

How far should you look into your future mate's finances?

If your future mate fails to discuss his financial income with you, would this prevent you from marrying them? Why or why not?

Situation #3 Generational Curses Revealed

Do you think that it is important to go around your potential mate's family and friends?

The Bible declares that marriage is honorable and the bed undefiled. Do you think that mates may go too far sexually in the bedroom, which causes them to go longing for things that may not be honorable to God or their mates? Discuss examples.

How would you handle the fact that your mate does not please you sexually?

How would you handle a sex addict?

How would you handle a generational curse that you learned about after you married your mate?

Situation #4 Convenience and Selfishness

How do you handle rejection?

How often should you allow yourself to be a rebound girl/boy? Or should you allow yourself to be a rebound girl/boy?

What are some of the signs in this situation that should have sent a flag to Sylvia that she was a rebound girl?

Why did Curtis hurt Sylvia?

Can a marriage of convenience last and be fulfilling?

Can a marriage with two selfish/self-centered people last?

Situation #5 Abuse

Is it ever acceptable to allow abuse in any form? Why or why not?

Why do people stay in abusive relationships?

Have you ever abused anyone and why did you do it?

Before the abuse goes too far, do we ever get any pre-warning signs that a person may be abusive?

Do you think that self-esteem has anything to do with the abused or the abuser?

Would you enter a relationship with a person who has a history of abuse?

Why or why not?

Another Marriage Situation – David, Nabal and Abigail

Bring this Bible Story up to our time and society.

Nabal was rich, but an ass. Do we sometimes marry for money?

Is that right or wrong?

What are some of the consequences of marrying solely for money?

Is it right that your potential mate go behind your back to fix a situation, even if it may benefit you in the long run? Could you handle that? How would it make you feel?

Further Questions to Discuss:

Have you set goals and standards to guide your relationship?

What would make you lower your standards?

Do you think when it comes to selecting a mate that we settle because of societal dictates (such as you are getting too old to be picky, there are 7 women to 1 man so you'd better hurry up. Man, you'd better marry her, she has everything you need – because woman usually have their own possessions, you'd better hurry up and get married so you can have children)?

Notes for Your Thoughts

Food for Thought-Marriage Quotes

"Marriage: Love is the reason. Lifelong friendship is the gift. Kindness is the cause. 'Til death do us part is the length." **Fawn Weaver**

"A successful marriage requires falling in love many times, always with the same person."
Mignon McLaughlin

"Being in a long marriage is a little bit like that nice cup of coffee every morning – I might have it every day, but I still enjoy it." **Stephen Gaines**

"Happily ever after is not a fairytale. It's a choice." - **Fawn Weaver**

"The older I get, the less time I want to spend with the part of the human race that didn't marry me." **Robert Brault**

"A happy marriage is the union of two good forgivers." - **Robert Quillen**

"The best time to love with your whole heart is always now, in this moment, because no breath beyond the current is promised." **-Fawn Weaver**

"To find someone who will love you for no reason, and to shower that person with reasons, that is the ultimate happiness." **Robert Brault**

"The difference between an ordinary marriage and an extraordinary marriage is in giving just a little 'extra' every day, as often as possible, for as long as we both shall live." **Fawn Weaver**

"We come to love not by finding a perfect person, but by learning to see an imperfect person perfectly." **-Sam Keen**

"Love doesn't make the world go 'round. Love is what makes the ride worthwhile."
Franklin P. Jones

"Where there is love, there is life." **Mahatma Gandhi**

"Marriage is a mosaic you build with your spouse. Millions of tiny moments that create your love story."
Jennifer Smith

"The greatest marriages are built on teamwork. A mutual respect, a healthy dose of admiration, and a never-ending portion of love and grace." **Fawn Weaver**

"Once we figured out that we could not change each other, we became free to celebrate ourselves as we are."
H. Dean Rutherford

(In a letter to his wife on their 59th wedding anniversary) "Love is the greatest gift when given. It is the highest honor when received." **Fawn Weaver**

"A long-lasting marriage is built by two people who believe in -and live by- the solemn promise they made."
-Darlene Schacht

"Coming together is a beginning; keeping together is progress; working together is success."
-Henry Ford

"A great marriage is not when the 'perfect couple' comes together. It is when an imperfect couple learns to enjoy their differences." **Dave Meurer**

"A great marriage isn't something that just happens; it's something that must be created."
Fawn Weaver

"Marriage is a commitment- a decision to do, all through life, that which will express your love for one's spouse."
Herman H. Kieval

"Show me a man who is smiling from ear-to-ear and living a beautiful life, and I'll show you a man who is grateful for what he has and utterly in love with his wife." **Fawn Weaver**

"A fool in love makes no sense to me. I only think you are a fool if you do not love." **Unknown**

"In the arithmetic of love, one plus one equals everything and two minus one equals nothing." **Mignon McLaughlin**

"Love is a partnership of two unique people who bring out the very best in each other, and who know that even though they are wonderful as individuals, they are even better together."
Barbara Cage

"The doors of happiness remain locked. When they are unlocked, they swing open quickly and widely but close right behind them. They must be reopened throughout each day and there is but one key that fits that lock: Gratitude." **Fawn Weaver**

"The first to apologize is the bravest. The first to forgive is the strongest. The first to forget is the happiest." **Unknown**

"Marriage is like watching the color of leaves in the fall, ever changing and more stunningly beautiful with each passing day." **Fawn Weaver**

"And in the end, the love you take is equal to the love you make."
John Lennon and Paul McCartney

"You meet thousands of people and none of them really touch you, and then you meet one person and your life is changed forever." **Jamie Randall (from the movie, Love and Other Drugs)**

"There are few things more frightening to a man than giving away his heart. And there are few things more comforting to a man than to know the woman he gave his heart to, will protect it with her life." **Fawn Weaver**

"Love is always bestowed as a gift -freely, willingly, and without expectation. We don't love to be loved, we love to love." **Leo Buscagalia**

"Love is an act of endless forgiveness, a tender look which becomes a habit." **Peter Ustinov**

"Passionate sex is great. A passionate marriage filled with passionate sex… SO much better."
Fawn Weaver

"Enjoy the little things in life… For one day you'll look back and realize they were the big things." **Kurt Vonnegut**

"Keep the fire lit in your marriage and your life will be filled with warmth." **Fawn Weaver**

Notes for Your Thoughts

Quotes About Learning From Mistakes

"We are products of our past, but we don't have to be prisoners of it."
— Rick Warren, *The Purpose Driven Life: What on Earth Am I Here for?*

"By seeking and blundering we learn."
— Johann Wolfgang von Goethe

"When a poet digs himself into a hole, he doesn't climb out. He digs deeper, enjoys the scenery, and comes out the other side enlightened."
— Criss Jami, *Venus in Arms*

"We do not learn from experience... we learn from reflecting on experience."
— John Dewey

The successful man will profit from his mistakes and try again in a different way."
— Dale Carnegie

"There are some things you can't learn at any university, except for one, the University of Life... the only college where everyone is a permanent student."
— E.A. Bucchianeri, *Brushstrokes of a Gadfly*

Fools say that they learn by experience. I prefer to profit by others experience."
— Otto von Bismarck

Many times what we perceive as an error or failure is actually a gift. And eventually we find that lessons learned from that discouraging experience prove to be of great worth."
— Richelle E. Goodrich, *Smile Anyway*

"No one is exempt from the rule that learning occurs through recognition of error."
— Alexander Lowen, *Bioenergetics*

"I am who I am today because of the mistakes I made yesterday."
— The Prolific Penman.

"We attract what we're meant to because we're aware & self-empowered enough to choose most of the time. Other times we have lessons to learn"
— Jay Woodman.

"Life is eventful which shapes our lives accordingly...."
— Fawad

"Past is treasure whether good or bad as both shape our lives, and shapeless things have no identity...."
— Fawad

"Our greatest mistakes, if we look at them, and digest them, and interact with them, and learn from them... they can be the greatest moments of our lives."
— Dan Pearce, *Single Dad Laughing*

The ideal of an "all-round" education is out of date. It has been destroyed by the progress of knowledge."
— Bertrand Russell, *Sceptical Essays*

"Failure is an Excuse, Success is a Choice." – Cynthia Turner

Coming soon to a bookstore near you...

A sneak preview just for you:

The First Ladies sat down together in Holysburg, PA reminiscing about their days as the First Lady at their individual churches. It was a long, hot summer day and they questioned themselves, how did we get here? Divorced in the church, Mercedes burst into tears. "I am so ashamed, it was not supposed to happen like this, he promised."

Paris angrily says, "Girl, shut the hell up, crying and mourning over that lump sack of..." Holy Ghost, help me. I just lost if for a minute.

Diamond stated, "Paris, you can be so insensitive at times. You need to let go of that bitterness, trying to be so strong on the outside, when you know inwardly that you are hurting just like us."

"No, I am not going to be a weakling like you girls, crying over spilled milk. It's over and I am moving on with my life and I suggest that you ladies do the same thing. But I promise you one thing, he will not get to act as if I don't exist. All of my life wasted, giving him babies and making sacrifices for the ministry. I was the valedictorian of my class, with a full scholarship, and I didn't even finish my degree, to help him build a ministry. I will be there every Sunday sitting on the front row, with my big hat, my fabulous suit, and with my mink around my shoulder. If he tries to get another wife on me, she will have something to contend with because I ain't, and I repeat, I ain't going nowhere. I will be right there in the Holy Ghost United for Christ Church for All People worshipping my Savior. I will see you ladies at another time. I think I need to go pray," Paris said.

Pearl could hardly wait until she got out of the door before she started talking about Paris. "She wants to be somebody's First Lady when she can't even bridle her tongue. All of that guile and insensitivity is coming out of her mouth. I feel sorry for her ex-husband because she needs some serious deliverance, unlike me, I am just holding on to God because he knows the plans he has for me so, I am going to let go and let God."

For Your Reading Pleasure, I recommend the Below Books for Spiritual Enlighten in Connection with the Information in this Book.

Suggested Readings

- Colson, Chuck, "Domestic Violence Within the Church: The Ugly Truth" BreakPoint October 20, 2009 http://www.christianheadlines.com/news/domestic-violence-within-the-church-the-ugly-truth-11602500.html
- Domestic Violence: Statistics & Facts, Get Help, http://www.dcadv.org/domestic-violence-facts-and-faqs
- Jones, Sheron, Heartache to Healing: Finding Grace Through God's Leading 2015
- Jakes, T. D., Let it Go Forgive So You Can Be Forgiven 2013
- Monroe, Myles, The Pursuit of Purpose. 1992
- NAWM, Holly Skinner, Marital Questionnaire. http://www.idovows.com/Premarital-Questionnaire.html
- Nash, Shirley, The Altars will Alter Your Life Forever 2010
- Shah, Bheekoo, "Top 10 Reasons Why Marriage Fails", http://www.onislam.net/english/family/special-coverage/464802-top-10-reasons-why-marriage-fails.html

- UF|CWC Counseling and Wellness Center, http://www.counseling.ufl.edu/cwc/Couples-intro.aspx
- Wilson, Barbara, "The Five Levels of Intimacy" January 16, 2014, http://thehartcentre.com.au/the-5-levels-of-intimacy-which-level-do-you-communicate-on/

Coming to a Book Store near you

To Walk Again
By: Kevin N. Washington
March 26, 1983-Automobile Accident Paralyzed-Only To Begin Walking November 1983

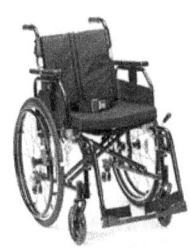

Be careful that you don't yoke yourself up with an ass.

About the Author

Cynthia is a native of Philadelphia, Pennsylvania. She is the youngest of eight siblings. She attends Gwynedd Mercy College when her schedule permits, and she is working on her Bachelor of Science Degree. She is a devout Christian believer and attends the Bethel Evangelistic Church of God in Christ, under the Pastorate of Elder George Nash Jr, where she serves in many capacities.

A Christian from her youth, she is a missionary and teaches sound doctrine. She is a lover of youth. Her motto is "A youth saved is a family saved" and one less person the devil can use to wreak havoc in the world. She is a Singles Advocate and has spoken at many Singles and Youth Ministry Workshops and services. She encourages young people to enjoy life before they plunge into marriage.

**The rings are given and the wedding plans are on the way.
The one thing a girl dreams of is
her well planned wedding day.**

**Finally, finally it's the wedding date.
Who would have ever thought that
their love would turn into hate?**

This book is a delightful reality that exposes the myth of marriage, deals with the reality of divorce within the religious and secular realm and challenges the divorced not to become the victim. It encourages persons to rise above the pain of failed relationships and marriages and not to hold the hurt that has been inflicted upon them as a result of bad relationship choices. This book is an encouragement to life after divorce. It is a teacher of acknowledging the error of your ways and moving on with your life after divorce. There is a caution on this book because the author goes outside the realm of religious dictates and tradition and dares to deal with poor relationships and failed marriages from the pulpit to the boardroom.

This book gives us a real up close depiction of relationships and the barriers that cause them to fail in the secular as well as Christian world.

Her prayer is that this book blesses you and causes you to avoid the pitfalls of yoking yourself up with an ass. She can be reached for speaking engagements and seminars at babygirlct07@gmail.com or babygirlct@outlook.com or babygirlct@comcast.net.

www.ingramcontent.com/pod-product-compliance
Lightning Source LLC
Chambersburg PA
CBHW070642160426
43194CB00009B/1544